"OH, NO!
He's Just Like My
FATHER"

Also by Sandra Reishus:

"Oh, No! I've Become My Mother"

"OH, NO! He's Just Like My FATHER"

Escape the Parent Trap & Have the Relationship YOU *Want*

SANDRA REISHUS, M.H.S.

Mc Graw Hill

New York Chicago San Francisco Lisbon London Madrid Mexico City
Milan New Delhi San Juan Seoul Singapore Sydney Toronto

The **McGraw·Hill** *Companies*

Library of Congress Cataloging-in-Publication Data

1 2 3 4 5 6 7 8 9 10 11 12 13 14 15   FGR/FGR   0 9 8 7

ISBN-13:   978-0-07-148236-3
ISBN-10:   0-07-148236-9

This book is printed on acid-free paper.

To my son,
David Ford,
With love and thanks for being the person you are

Contents

Acknowledgments

Thank you to everyone at McGraw-Hill for the interest, support, and enthusiasm for my books. I appreciate everyone in each department that my book goes through. Design, production, publicity, marketing, and sales—thanks a million for all your great work.

My editor, Johanna Bowman, was a delight to work with. Her comments were always right-on, and her attention to detail helped make this book clearer and more concise. She saw exactly where to add and where to subtract, and I am grateful for her editing skills. A great big thank-you, Johanna.

My angel agent, Joelle Delbourgo, continues to be right there, encouraging and supporting all my literary efforts. It's always fun and informational talking to you on the phone and having you share your humor, your wisdom, and your stories with me. A big kiss and hug to you, Joelle.

My granddaughter, Hailey Margaret, who just keeps getting sweeter and cuter each day, is one of the highlights of my life. We have such great "girl time" together, whether it's being theater buddies, going shopping, or just hanging out.

You are so creative and intelligent, and I'm looking forward to seeing how that develops. We are definitely soul sisters forever. You are the best.

Dai, I want to thank you for your sensitivity, that dry sense of humor that is you, your compassion, and your insight into people and life. I've watched you grow and mature, and it's been wonderful to see you become the great person that you are today. We've been able to move our parent-child relationship to a friendship that is very special to me. You have taught me so much, and for that, I am forever grateful. I was truly blessed the day you were born.

Thanks to my brother, Dave Reishus, and sister-in-law, Diane Young, for keeping Christmas a family affair. This is one couple who got their relationship right!

Thanks to Marianne McKusick, Dana Jefferey, and everyone who understood when they called and wanted me to do something and I said I had to write. Thanks to you, Colette Adcock, for understanding when I didn't write e-mails very often; it was because I had my head full of the book.

A big thanks to Ron Cisneros, my dance teacher. I love your Broadway jazz classes—which allow me to get out of my head and back into my body, keeping me in balance—and your sense of humor always brings a smile to my face. I'll be there as long as you are!

Richard, you are always there with just the right words and off-the-wall funny comments for which I am forever grateful. I wouldn't be where I am without you.

And to all my clients, friends, and acquaintances, thanks for the trust you have placed in me. You have enriched my life and enhanced this book with all that you've shared. I couldn't have done it without you!

Introduction

Get ready, because what you're about to read will change your life. Whether you're single, married, or somewhere in between, it's important to know and fully understand how and why you make the choices you do in your selection of romantic relationship partners. The surprise is that, much of the time, we unconsciously allow our past relationships with our parents to make our choices. Of course, that's the last thing anyone wants to hear, and when they do, they usually say, "Maybe someone else did, but not me." The vast majority of people would strongly defend the conviction that their parents had nothing to do with their choice of partner.

This common belief is usually expressed as "Of course, we make our own choices. Our parents aren't arranging our marriages like in the old days! I looked and looked and rejected lots of people who didn't meet my criteria until I found what I was looking for." Sure, most of us might have shopped around for The One, but what we don't often realize is that our choices were limited because we were subconsciously looking for a person who was uncannily like Mom or Dad. That "love is blind" saying certainly holds true and goes undetected on our "He's the One" radar.

If you believe you've chosen someone who doesn't look or act like your dad, you just might wake up one morning with the realization, "Oh, my gosh! Last night at dinner my husband flirted with my girlfriend the whole time. I thought I was the only one he used his seductive ways on and I was special to him, but apparently not. Mom divorced Dad for the affairs he had, and here I am looking at that same possibility in my marriage. Am I headed down the same path, and how did I end up with what seems to be the same situation? How did I ever get here?"

When you're deciding who Mr. Right is, you don't even realize you are re-creating a relationship that might date back to when you were growing up. This book takes you beyond the obvious similarities you might see between your father and your partner, such as looks, career, personality, level of sensitivity, or the conviction that the toilet paper should roll up or down. Take a deep breath, because we're going deeper to find the similarities that are more difficult to recognize and are at the heart of the parent trap.

With this new information, there's a big shocker—realizing that you can't always depend on chemistry to make good decisions. After the initial passion has cooled, many women realize (sometimes too late) that they've married their father, and many men figure out that the woman they've wed is Mom in disguise. This book will show you the whys and hows of mate selection, as well as how to escape the parent trap and make real, unhindered choices without the mom-and-dad baggage. If you're already in a relationship, great! Now you'll have the information you need to change yourself and your relationship for the better or to move on to better things. Escaping the parent trap is all about finding options.

It may come as news or you might have figured it out already, but building and maintaining relationships are among the hardest things we do in life. We all want wonderful ones in which we can be who we are and have the other person respect and honor that. Now you can get on the road toward this goal.

The Parent Trap Defined

It would be quite an education if, as children, we moved from one family to another, seeing all the different types of marital relationships and parental styles. We would see people who worked well together as couples and those who didn't. We would see sensitive parents, insensitive parents, and all of the degrees between. I'm not saying that this would be a good thing or a desirable childhood, but think about all the different views of life we would be exposed to and the options we would have in determining our sense of self and the way we deal with relationships.

One family might see us as intelligent or ambitious or generous, whereas another might see us as underachieving or aimless or self-centered. One family might be able to work through their problems calmly, whereas another yelled all the time or gave each other the silent treatment. We'd have a kaleidoscope of choices for what we believed about ourselves and how to have the best relationships. Maybe the Browns showed us how to walk away from a fight and come back later to resolve the issue. The Smiths showed us the lighter, fun side of life, and the Joneses' showed us how to manipulate people (a behavior we knew we didn't want to emulate).

In theory this would be great, but in reality we were only exposed to one way of seeing the world and have internalized the various messages about ourselves and relationships that we received from our caregivers and their way of dealing with life. We carry those views around with us wherever we go, and we can't escape them or remain immune to their influence in our lives. These messages have worn such a deep groove in our brains that we often fail to recognize when they are running our lives. Acting these messages out, whether, consciously or subconsciously, is what I refer to as the parent trap. We're trapped in the cycle of doing things our parents' way or in reaction to their messages about us rather than exploring our own options in relationships—and we're stuck in the trap until we can free ourselves. The parent trap can affect us in unexpected ways:

- We're attracted to the familiarity of childhood because it's comfortable, so we choose mates who are similar to our fathers with both the positive and negative traits.
- We find someone, anyone, to fill those voids in our lives left by our parents.
- We re-create our parent's relationship in our own lives either by doing the same thing or by rebelling and doing the exact opposite—which is just a different side of the same coin.
- We pick up our love fantasies from our parents and attempt to live them out, not realizing that we are building castles in the sand rather than living in reality.
- We carry our coping mechanisms from childhood—which we used to save us from our fear of loneliness,

isolation, abuse, or anything we couldn't handle as a child—into our adult relationships, thereby thwarting true intimacy.

- We choose certain interpersonal dynamics not because they fit our needs, but because they perpetuate the only relationship style in which we feel safe and protected.

The good news here is that you don't have to stay stuck. The way to free yourself from any parent trap is, first, to gather information on what parental messages and views you hang onto; second, to conduct an introspective look at how they play out in your life; and third, to move forward into change. You will learn about all of this in the following chapters. Stay tuned for your informative ride down the relationship road! It will never look the same again.

Relationship Theories

Some of the theories I'll refer to have been around for decades, but rarely does anyone break them down using easy-to-understand language. That's what I'll do—along with offering some new advice on how you can discover the true nature of your relationship with your partner and get rid of the overshadowing influence of your parents.

Freud believed that we marry our parents; Jung's theory was that we marry someone with the qualities we lack; and Gloria Steinem—bless her soul—told us that we become the man we want to marry by developing the qualities we want to find in our men. For example, if we are looking for a successful man, we then become successful ourselves. Although all three ideas have legitimate points, I throw my hat in

Freud's ring because I have seen my clients prove it true time after time. When I mention this subject to friends or strangers, it always elicits a laugh and a story starting with, "Let me tell you about this relationship I had (or have)." While some people can see the reality of Freud's theory, it's still hidden in the trenches of others' subconscious. When it is finally uncovered, there is a light-bulb moment that makes them aware of why they chose certain partners. It's an awakening to hidden agendas that can then be explored and resolved.

Freud, in all his wisdom, could see that we choose a partner who will let us re-create the relationship we had with a parent in our earlier years, whether that relationship met most of our needs or was sorely lacking. For example, if Dad was abusive in any way, we will probably hook up with a man who is also abusive; if Dad handled us with kid gloves and made our life one big party, then that will be what attracts us when we're looking for a romantic partner.

Our father was *the man* in our lives during all of our formative years, whether he was present or deserted us and was simply acknowledged as the sperm donor. Adult romantic relationships can be traced to a tie-in to what we liked and didn't like about our first role model of the male of the species. On the other hand, it could be Mom we choose as a mate down the road so we can work out our issues with her by proxy.

Although this book discusses the correlation between fathers and the mates we choose, we could also have chosen someone just like Mom in our partner selection. If that's the case for you, then substitute the word *mother* for *father*. Or you might see you have chosen someone who has characteristics and dynamics of both Mom and Dad. This is very common, so you'll want to keep that in mind as you read through the book and take the quizzes. Occasionally, we just choose one or the other, but looking deeper, we can find a common ground the two of them had whether it was lack of sensitivity, a focus on the family as an ideal rather than on each individual, or an emotional unavailability.

Neither of my parents was emotionally available—gee, I wonder why they chose each other—so for a long time, I kept picking men who were not accessible either. That was my norm growing up, so I continued the pattern until I learned to look at men and determine whether they were stand-ins for my parents. It made all the difference in the world. Many times, this concept seems obvious but isn't until we are fully educated on the tendencies of the parent trap. Until we have that "light-bulb moment," we're in the dark.

Who This Book Is For

This book is for everyone who has had a romantic relationship, is currently involved in one, or is looking to get into one. For those of you who are single and are currently looking for a relationship or want to have one in the future, this will give you a heads-up on what you should be looking for, both within yourself and in your potential partner. It will give you supportive information so you don't fall for the first man who turns your head. You'll be a step ahead of the game, allowing you to bypass any heartbreak that would have come your way if you went into the relationship blindly, as most of us do until we get smarter about our patterns.

If you are in a relationship but haven't quite decided if marriage is the next step, you will learn how to tell if your partner is really someone you should legally settle down with. You don't want to waste either your energy or your time if you'll eventually look back and say, "What was I thinking? Where was my head? I feel like I was deaf, dumb, and blind to have missed the red flags that were flying all over this relationship." This book will answer those questions for you and give you insight into all future relationships you might consider so that you don't have to repeat the same scenario over again.

If you are in a committed relationship, you will learn why you and your partner are at odds over various subjects. You will look at what and why you are contributing what you are to the relationship and understand the same about your partner. Having this information can help you become more compatible and heal long-standing wounds. All it takes is introspection on both your parts and a willingness to grow as a person and a partner. You will also gain insight about whether you should stay in your relationship or not.

What You Can Expect from This Book

If many of us look closely at relationships we have had in the past or are currently involved in, we will see that we have uncannily chosen someone who is either just like one of our parents or a blend of both of them to make it just a little more confusing. We are playing out a scenario from our childhood, making us unable to leave the past behind and move forward in the area of love and relationships. The similarity may not be obvious at first, but with learned insight, you will find a connection. You just might see that your workaholic honey is no different than Mom, who watched soap operas all day. Both were "checked-out" on an emotional level, even though they looked completely different on the surface. Once you have an insight into the role your parents played in your selection, you will begin to see the larger picture, which consists of the following:

- How you deal with the present based on your past conditioning
- The similarities between your parents and your mate
- How relationship myths can be banished
- How sabotage and coping mechanisms work
- How to avoid fear-based relationships
- Why chemistry isn't always a good thing in all decisions
- How you can learn to move on to a rewarding relationship
- The signs of a healthy versus an unhealthy relationship

You can use this knowledge in the relationship you have now, or if you are on the lookout for a relationship, you can use it to ensure that you are not operating on past beliefs. In either case, it can help you move toward your goal of having the best relationship possible. If you are enlightened and free of the parent trap, you will always be putting your best foot forward.

With my clients, both male and female, I've seen a growing interest in "why" they chose the romantic partners they did. Everyone wants answers so they can sort it all out, and this perspective gives them a starting place. A door opens for them, and at long last their relationship starts to make sense. I love when the light bulb goes on, and it becomes clear that they have made the connection. I can see it in their eyes, and they say, "Oh, that makes perfect sense" or "I get it" or "That explains a lot." Then they can start to unravel the intricacies of their interpersonal connections and move on to healthier, happier relationships.

This book will give you quizzes, exercises, and checklists so you can address your unique experiences, concerns, and goals in an interactive way. Not only will it guide you to interpret, analyze, and finally understand your role in relationships, but it will also help you learn to laugh at yourself—and if it's a good day, maybe even with your parents and your partner.

Chemistry Doesn't Work in the Long Run

Why We Are Less-than-Savvy Shoppers When Choosing a Mate

We think we choose a partner for looks, sense of humor, stability, or excitement. Or we may look for a type: tall, dark, and handsome or short, witty, and cute. To some extent, this is true, but there is more at play than just simple attraction and the romance of Cupid's arrow. Of course, we're driven by our desire to find everlasting love. We are so starstruck—and we should be—by the power of love that often we do not consider the other factors that influence our selection of The One. Now, I'm not suggesting that you don't love the person you're with or that love isn't part of why you chose him. But many times, besides bringing wonderful and fabulous things to a relationship, love can also cloud your perception so that you might not see the other reasons you chose this person.

While we believe we pick our mate based on love, underneath that feeling there is a psychological process of which we are unaware. Is someone taking over our body and making these decisions for us? No, but we are not aware of the real reasons we are making them. This process goes on far below the conscious level at which we experience our mundane, day-to-day activities that govern our behavior, leading us to select one person over another.

Understanding this phenomenon will open many doors for you that have been closed. You have been blocked from incorporating new opportunities into your life, but that's all going to change. You will learn the what, why, and how of relationships and give yourself options you never had before.

Let's say you want a new pair of shoes and only know of one store that carries the ones you want. Then you find out that two other stores carry the pair you like. One store is close and very expensive. Another store is twenty miles away, but the price tag on the shoes says fifty dollars less than at the first place. The third store has a great knock-off pair at half price, but it's in the next town. If you didn't know about the second two options, you would only have one store to choose from, and you certainly wouldn't be a savvy shopper. But by finding out that there are other stores with the merchandise you want, your eyes are opened to the many options out there, and you can make an informed decision about where to make your purchase.

Let's apply the savvy-shopper metaphor to choosing The One. Understanding what leads us to our partner choices allows us to pick a person who will meet our current needs on a personal level rather than carrying forward our emotional baggage from the past. By seeing this baggage clearly, we find we have choices in mate selection that we've never had before, just like shopping for those shoes. You can now become an enlightened, savvy shopper when choosing a mate or remaking the relationship you're already in.

One Piece of the Puzzle

What I have found, both personally and professionally, is that we uncannily choose to be around people who are just like Mom or Dad, but we may have difficulty making the connection because they look different in a lot of ways. Perhaps your parents only graduated from high school and the man you are interested in has a graduate degree, or your family is in the upper crust of society and his is from the working class. They may look different, but underneath the link is there just the same. There are going to be similarities between your parents and your beau that show up over time. Maybe you'll discover that regardless of how much education he has, he can still be insensitive. Or the fact that one family has more money than another doesn't mean that the wealthy people are more honest and trustworthy.

JESSICA:
LOOKING FOR LOVE,
BUT MISSING THE POINT

Jessica spent time in biker bars in hopes of meeting an interesting, exciting, fun man. Her parents were narrow-minded, conservative people, and she knew they didn't have a good relationship because there were so many arguments in the house. She decided she was going to live her life differently and find someone free-spirited and nonconformist. She figured that was better than the one-dimensional life she had with her parents growing up. That had been duty-driven and prone to fighting. She was expected to clean her room daily, do the dishes every night, feed the dog every morning, wash clothes three times a week, and cook dinner on a regular basis by the time she was eight. If she missed any of those chores, she was yelled at, told she wasn't contributing to the family, and was selfish.

She wanted to get as far away from that as she could manage. She craved excitement and adventure, and now that she was living on her own, she had already had some great experiences with friends she had made at the bars. When one of these friends introduced her to George, she was quite taken with him and the exciting life he had. He didn't really live anywhere. Sometimes he spent the night in one state, sometimes in another; he stayed with friends, camped out, or spent money for a room. It was such a different lifestyle that she was immediately attracted to it. The point she missed was that he was at the other extreme from her parents: they lived in a narrow world, but so did George. He only worked when he needed the money; he picked up and took off when the notion hit him; and nothing was going to make him change. He had looked so different when she met him, but she began to see that she had chosen the same type of situation, just a different side of the same coin. Her parents were extreme, he was extreme, and neither took her feelings into consideration. It was their way or the highway.

Until we make the connection between our parents and the men we select, we won't be savvy shoppers. Instead, we are stuck making the same relationship choices over and over.

According to divorce statistics, one out of two marriages doesn't make it long term. We need to look at the reasons this happens. The majority of people believe at the beginning of their relationship that this one is "different" and are convinced, without a doubt, that theirs is a match made in heaven. Some of those people are right, but if we take into account the 50 percent who stay together for reasons other than marital bliss—such as "for the sake of the children" (I've never had clients be thankful their parents stayed together for their sake, which tells you something), financial stability, or because they are afraid of facing life alone—the statistics are not in favor of a wonderful marriage. The fact is there needs to be more understanding of what influences relationships and how we carry baggage (good and bad) into our partnerships. These concepts are paramount to bringing happiness into our lives.

The Present Won't Fix the Past

The first and most fundamental reason for disharmony in relationships is that we are subconsciously trying to heal our past. We're re-creating it in the present, trying to fix the flaws of our childhood in the here and now. Unfortunately, this is like trying to go back and not have that broken arm at age six. It simply can't be done.

If you want to know the injuries that were inflicted on you in childhood, you have to look at the relationships you have today. You will either end up with someone who is just like your parents, or you will rebel against your parents and end up with the exact opposite, which is equally damaging.

For example, if you were always afraid of rejection as a child, you may now live with feelings of separation and the fear of getting too close. This can manifest as being with someone who isn't really emotionally in the relationship; he's there in body only, but there's emotional distance between the two of you. Conversely, if your mother always forgot to pick you up at school, you might marry a man who clings to you until you can hardly breathe. If presents were sparse and Christmas was a downer in your childhood, you may now give a five-page list of what you want to your honey, expecting to make up for the lackluster holidays you remember. But all the presents in the world aren't going to erase your past wants, needs, and desires.

Sometimes we attempt to rectify the past through the present over and over with different relationships, and sometimes we keep trying with the same person, even though we get identical results. Whether you are stuck in this pattern with different people or the same one, the past doesn't change, and you are left with unmet needs. You thought a relationship would be one of life's answers, but it seems to have failed the test.

The first step toward having a satisfying relationship is to understand what you have been trying to do that isn't working and seeing clearly the futility of your old mission. Know that there are voids that were created in childhood by Mom or Dad and that you unknowingly try to fill those voids by selecting someone who is like one or both of your parents. Only then can you have a successful, new mission by taking responsibility for your own actions and the relationships you have created. Only then can you start to move into your adult life free from anything that binds you to the past.

A Word on Blame

Don't look at this as dissing your parents; we are not blaming them for being who they were. They had their own struggles growing up, and most of the time, they did the best they could in raising you based on their own past. They are not guilty parties, and we are not going to string them up for what they've done, but you have to look at how they operated in their relationship in the most objective way possible to see the effects their behavior had on you.

We *all* have wounds to our psyche from childhood because our parents, by the very nature of being human, were less-than-perfect models of behavior in some way. Remember, there are no perfect parents. Perfection is a myth fostered by the media and has done us a lot of harm. Let's let go of that notion right here. Imperfection is a good thing. Think about what it would be like to be raised by a parent who was "perfect" in every way (even if that were possible) and what you'd have to live up to. What a disaster that would be—you'd have to stock up on Ben and Jerry's by the freezerfull for all the stress-induced eating you'd want to do. A perfect parent would certainly create much more massive adult issues than those you are dealing with now, so thank your lucky stars it's a myth.

Even if your parents had a great relationship, there were still dynamics between them that could have been better. Just as there are no perfect parents, there are no perfect marriages, either. All relationships go through phases of compatibility and disconnect. This can be caused by outside influences such as unemployment, job stress, an accident or illness, the death of someone close, or a move to another location.

Perhaps our parents were grieving or scared or uprooted or their confidence had been shaken. Going through these life events is all part of being a couple, but it does have a bearing on what messages we picked up from our parents as they were dealing with these issues. They might have been in a good place when your brother was young, but when you came along, Dad may have lost his job and life became more complicated. What you saw and later re-created in your own life depends on where they were when you were growing up.

Carol and Gene: It's the 1950s All Over Again

Carol met her future husband at a friend's house. Her friend was cooking an elaborate meal and invited her brother-in-law, Gene. It came as quite a surprise to the hosts when Carol and Gene seemed to hit it off and started dating. Within three months, they had moved in together and then made plans to get married. The families had met and seemed to get along well enough, so all was well in their world. Carol didn't know that she should look at Gene's parents and the type of relationship they had to determine what her future husband's expectations were going to be.

In the first year of their marriage, she had a little boy and was a stay-at-home mom while Gene pursued his career in advertising. When their son started school, Carol expressed a desire to rejoin the workforce. She was missing the camaraderie of coworkers and wanted to be back in the adult world. Gene was adamant that she stay home and wouldn't hear a word about her going back to work. The case was closed as far as he was concerned.

One day it struck Carol that she was making dinner, putting it on the table, calling Gene away from the computer to eat, clearing the table, and by agreement, waiting for him to clean up the dishes in the kitchen. Most of the time, he got up from the table and went right back to the computer, deciding to clean up maybe later that night and possibly even waiting until the next day. Carol started looking at his parents' marriage, and lo and behold, there was the explanation. His mom did the cooking, cleaning, and child rearing while his father went to his office, played golf, or hung around with his cronies. Come to think of it, her own father went to work, came home, hung out, and went to bed, only to do it all again the next day. She had married her father, and her husband thought he had married his mom. It could have gone on forever, except that Carol didn't want a relationship like either of their parents had. It became clear to her that she had to move on with her life and find out who she was outside of the expectation that her only worth was as a traditional housewife.

Repeating the Past Is Comfortable

We are always attracted to the familiar because it is comfortable and we know how to handle it. You would think that if the familiar weren't good for us, we would run the other way and yes, consciously we try to do that. But unconsciously we still seek it out. That we would get involved in a situation that wasn't in our best interests doesn't make much sense on the surface, yet the parallels between our current relationship and what we experienced growing up are always there. If we were yelled at a lot in childhood, you would think we'd search for the opposite and find someone nice and quiet who wouldn't raise his voice in a million years. But what we might not see is that subconsciously we equate displeasure with caring. Our partner doesn't yell, but a look or shrug of the shoulder gives us that same disapproval message.

What we know feels a lot less scary than what we don't know. Comfort is a cage. It may not get us what we want in a relationship, but it's a safe place to be. This is why women often choose to hook up with abusive men. They've had some form of abuse in their past and know what to expect. Most of us don't want the rug suddenly pulled out from under us or to be blindsided by something we're not expecting, so we choose familiarity.

RUTH AND JIM: RE-CREATING THEIR CHILDHOODS AS ADULTS

Ruth grew up with a father who disapproved of her, so she took into adult life the belief that there was something wrong with her. She married Jim, who was a disapproving person, but she didn't consciously see the similarities. She did, however, know how to deal with him, just as she had learned to deal with her dad.

When Dad would tell her the outfit she was wearing was inappropriate (even though everyone else was wearing the same thing and the school wasn't objecting), she simply ignored him and went on her merry way. She had internalized the message though, and it left a void in her. She had needed her dad's approval and instead had gotten rejection. When Jim told her she was too loud when she drank around his friends, she simply smiled and continued, not giving any credence to what he said. She knew how to get by this verbal bullet because she'd been doing it all her life. It was comfortable because she knew how to handle it. But at the same time, she hoped that she could get Jim's approval on everything she did, which would mean her dad was mistaken in criticizing her and there really wasn't anything wrong with her. That would fix the negative messages from childhood, and she'd finally feel like a worthwhile person.

Jim, on the other hand, couldn't support who she was as a person because that wasn't the way he was raised. In his family, compliments weren't given; his parents said that you could remedy shortcomings by pointing them out and that critiques only made you a better person. His parents were the judge and jury of his behavior, just as he was of Ruth's behavior. There was no way he could reverse his upbringing and give her what she craved. He thought he was doing something helpful, but her voids remained.

Conveniently, if subconsciously, we think we can choose a replica of Mom or Dad to heal the past and get rid of all the hurts we experienced when we were young. Because this type of relationship is a known quantity, we can operate with some degree of ease. A part of us thinks we just killed two birds with one stone. What we don't see is the downside of never having our true needs met. I tell my clients that it's like walking around with holes in our psyches. You may love beauty, but you don't allow yourself to have it because your parents gave you the message that you aren't good enough. If you were taught not to trust anyone, you walk around with a hole representing mistrust. You want to trust and look to others to fill that hole, but they can only do so much. Eventually you are the only one who can fill it. Being comfortable with a relationship simply because the dynamics feel familiar isn't going to get you very far in healing your past and emerging as a truly self-confident person.

Your Mate's Parent Trap

In any type of relationship, the two people involved can only go as far as the most limited one. For example, you can't make a man be more sensitive than he is, so you are pretty much stuck with whatever level he can go to. As much as you might like the relationship to have lots of empathy and understanding, it isn't going to happen because he is what he is in this area and that's all he's got.

Also, he brings good and bad baggage to the relationship based on his parent trap just as you do. When you think about it, most of us can tell within the first ten minutes of meeting a man how much money he wants you to believe he has. If he talks about what kind of car he drives or where he lives, or he makes sure you see that he leaves a large tip after dinner or that twenty platinum credit cards fall out of his wallet, you know he wants you to believe he has plenty of disposable income. When you have sex with him for the first time, you are going to find out if anyone has ever asked him to wear a condom before and whose pleasure he's most interested in. You are getting clues from him all the time on what he believes about you, himself, and relationships. If you are smart enough to pick up on these signs, you are going to learn a lot, and it's all to your benefit in determining whether he's your dream man or one to throw back in the water for someone else to catch.

If you've married this man, you are going to find out in that important first year how his idea of being a husband differs from his idea of being a boyfriend. Maybe there is just a subtle change, and that's great for you. On the other hand, you could wonder when the aliens made the switch and gave you this person instead of your old boyfriend. Getting to the nitty-gritty, the most important thing you are going to find out in the first year of marriage is his thinking on whether the two of you should turn into his mom and dad. You just might be surprised at how often he does believe this. Sometimes it's buried deep inside of him, and he doesn't even know he felt that you and he should live just like his parents did, but now it's surfacing for you and him to deal with.

Just as you look at your own parents to illuminate your relationship choices and behavior, you have to look at his parents to see what kind of messages he picked up along the way from his family and what parental messages he's operating under. They're different and have to be viewed independently. You can't use your family system to predict his behavior because pasts are not interchangeable.

He might think you should be like his mom, and he may start turning into his dad, but maybe that's not your idea of a great relationship. Always look at his role models in this area and see if you think you can live with at least some of them, because they will show up somewhere along the way.

The Skinny on Re-Creating Parents' Relationship Models, Dynamics, and Fantasies

In later chapters you will learn more detail about the ins and outs of the parent trap, but for now, let's look at some broad definitions of what constitutes that trap.

Relationship Models

Our parents were our role models for relationships when we were young and impressionable and only part of our brain was developed. We weren't given lots of choices on how relationships could be handled, so the one we were exposed to became our norm. In some cases, the picture had lots of positives in it, and in other cases, it left a lot to be desired in the quest for a happy, healthy partnership.

It's similar to learning only one language as we grew up. If we weren't exposed to other languages, we had no choice but to speak the one we were taught. Most of our parents only spoke one language, just as they only portrayed one way of being in relationships. In this regard, we held them up as the model of how coupling is done and accepted that as gospel—at least in our formative years. After we got older, we might have questioned their behavior, but by then a certain wiring had occurred in our brains by repeatedly seeing how they conducted their relationship. That wiring affects how we conduct our own as adults.

Relationship Dynamics

This is how we relate to each other and the roles we play in each and every relationship we forge. Our dynamic could be that one partner is the funny person and the other laughs at his or her jokes, or it could be that one partner isn't expected to actively participate in family outings and the other is fine with that. Or the dynamic could be on a deeper level, such as who has the power and control in the relationship and who plays the martyr or victim. The dynamic we have with our mate is often unspoken and is the way the two of us feel comfortable being in a relationship because we have experienced it before in childhood.

You fall into re-creating parental dynamics without even realizing you have done it. Dynamics are usually set up in the first stages of a relationship and become permanent fixtures, so be careful when forming a new relationship that you aren't going to regret it down the road when it's going to be very difficult to change. For example, if you are expected to call when you get home after your date together and you comply, you are on your way to setting up a dynamic of playing into your boyfriend's irrational fears that something is going to happen to you and he won't hear about it until the police come knocking on his door. All of a sudden, he has taken control of this relationship and you have allowed it. More likely than not, one of your parents also exerted unnecessary control over the other or over you, and you are repeating their dynamic as this is what you were exposed to and internalized at a young age.

Fantasies

The idea that love is going to solve all our problems and our knight in shining armor is going to arrive in the nick of time to make our lives wonderful is a complete fantasy that we develop in childhood. There's no doubt that Cinderella had a dysfunctional family, but rather than looking at reality and how *she* could change her situation, Prince Charming came to the rescue and they lived happily ever after. Couple the fairytales you grew up with and any emotional wounds you received from your parents, and you have created some far-reaching romantic fantasies.

Even if we didn't see a healthy, working relationship in our youth, we did see the happy endings in stories, so we know just how to make our lives wonderful and devoid of any strife: find the right man. Oh, if only that were true. We need to sleuth out the fantasies we are operating under and put them in the recycling bin so we can have a real chance at a wonderful relationship. More on that later.

Karen and Paul: Choosing the Opposite Brings Them Closer to the Same

Karen had a dad who was married to his career. It was hard growing up that way, as she always thought there must be something wrong with her and that was the reason he was never around much. She always tried to be the best little girl possible, hoping he would want to spend more time with her, but it never worked. She didn't know what she was doing wrong and blamed herself for his disinterest in her.

When she was old enough to start thinking about marriage and having children of her own, she knew she didn't want them to have a dad like hers. Her dream man would spend time with her and value the family life they shared. That was what was most important to her, and she set her sights on one man in particular whom she had met playing tennis. Paul seemed to fit the picture; he was a mellow, laid-back kind of man. Karen didn't know that he was looking for a wife who would not push him to do more than he wanted, like his own demanding father had done. He wanted a nice, easy, calm life without any drama or trauma in it and came across as a caring individual. But to Karen, he seemed to be just what the doctor ordered.

The trouble began shortly after they were married. Sure, he would stick around the house and didn't have many outside interests, but being involved in much of anything that was couple-oriented was beyond his scope. At the beginning, it looked like a match made in heaven, but that didn't last long. Karen thought having children would involve him more and help create the life she was looking for. Maybe she couldn't get a lot of his attention, but surely children would do the trick.

Unfortunately, he wasn't able to relate to his children any more than he was able to relate to Karen, and when he did, it was to send a message of disapproval. When Karen saw he really didn't take much of a personal interest in her or the family they had started, she begged and pleaded with him to be more involved. When he didn't comply, she began to nag and get angry at him, resulting in many fights. Paul was in the same position he had been in with his dad; he saw Karen as demanding. He had married his father, the same as Karen had. She was again involved with a man who was not there in any meaningful way. They each had unconsciously chosen a parent, and it didn't work any better in their marriage than it had in their childhood. There was no way it could have worked because their past issues hadn't been resolved. They are now in counseling and trying to work out this dynamic, but it looks like it's going to be a long haul getting from where they are to where they want to be.

The Chemistry Factor: Fact or Fiction?

You think you've met the man of your dreams. He's good-looking, kind, sweet, generous, apparently sensitive, and your heart is beating a mile a minute. You have this chemistry together, and just looking into his eyes or hearing his voice on the phone is enough to send you into another time and place. To top that off, he feels the same way. Nothing matters to you but being with him. You believe this must be love because of all the adrenaline running through your body. You know it's meant to be and you will live happily ever after.

This scenario sounds like a movie plot, but you haven't yet seen that below the surface his sensitivity is only skin-deep, his good looks have allowed him to be a big-time flirt, and his generosity carries a price tag. Once you set the chemistry aside, you begin to see the total package. And suddenly, it dawns on you: he's just like your mom or dad! You've fallen into the parent trap. You knew on some level that he was familiar. Dad appeared to be sensitive also, but what about him giving you the nickname "klutz" when you were young? And then there's Mom, who would do anything for you as long as you thought she was the most wonderful person alive, but when you didn't, it was all taken away.

You thought, subconsciously, that this was your chance to redo your childhood and fill those voids left by your parents. This time it was going to work, or so the magical thinking went. This man was going to be sensitive without inflicting any hurts, and he was going to be generous without expecting something in return and making it a manipulative situation. He was going to have what you wanted from your parents and didn't get. But the idea of the perfect mate is still a fantasy.

But what are you supposed to do when you meet someone who takes your breath away? How should you react when all your hormones go into overdrive, you get all tingly inside, and you can't stop thinking about this man? You just know he is the one for you because you don't always feel this way; the chemistry is telling you it's true, and who's to argue with chemistry? Emerson says, "Love is strongest in pursuit, friendship in possession," which means that particular chemicals are the strongest at the start of a relationship and wane thereafter.

This initial phase usually lasts, on average, from eighteen months to three years and gives way to the attachment phase which involves a different chemical system. At the beginning of the first phase, neurons in the limbic system of the brain become either saturated or sensitized by natural amphetamines—phenylethylamine along with dopamine and norepinephrine—which is what gives you those feelings of "Oh, this is the best relationship I've ever had," or "He's the absolute one," or even "I can't live without him." It's the closest you can get to a natural high, but you have to beware of what you're missing in all this euphoria.

One of the problems of having these chemical reactions is that you tend to avoid looking closely at the rest of the relationship and, instead, glory in the feelings produced. You may be in love with the chemical feeling and not with who that man really is. If you are a relationship junkie, this may be the feeling you are looking for, and you run from one relationship to another, wanting to feel it time after time. That's one way to live, but if you are looking for something long term, there are other things to take into consideration.

Remember that you have to take the whole package and not just the parts you like. If you don't look at the whole kit and caboodle, you are missing some important messages. If you love and focus on his intelligence, you might miss that he's really self-centered or insensitive or angry or has lots of baggage of his own that will interfere with any and all relationships.

Love takes time to grow—years, in fact—so don't mistake the initial rush or endorphin overload as the real thing when it's simply infatuation. Many of us have had the experience of an intense sexual attraction to someone who we either found out down the road wasn't relationship material or we knew that in the beginning, but couldn't get past the sex high. It can be that right after sex we wondered why we went ahead and participated when now we have to face the light of day without our libido getting in the way. If it doesn't hit us right away, that emerges at some point, maybe the next day or the next time we have a fight. Most of us know what is happening but are powerless to stop, at least until we get our heads on straight.

It was almost like an addiction that we couldn't control, but that's all the relationship had going for it that worked that well. Sometimes it's hard to separate the reality from the sexual draw, but remember you still have to deal with your partner out of bed, and with some people, that simply can't be done in a healthy way no matter what our chemicals say.

At the start of a "made-in-heaven" relationship, it feels like everything is going to be wonderful, but taking a closer look reveals that you experienced these same dynamics a long, long time ago. The idea that chemistry means love is really a dip into the past. Although this new insight takes away some of the excitement of meeting someone with whom you have great chemistry, it saves you from future heartache. So, always look behind the scenes to make sure you aren't re-creating or reacting to your past. Since we seek out in our adult relationships what we experienced as children—whether that was advantageous to us or not—be afraid, be very afraid of that same dynamic showing up as instant attraction.

My advice in all of this is if you have an instant connection with someone and your chemicals go haywire, turn around and run the other way because you've just met your past. It may not seem like it, but this feeling could be speaking to you loud and clear if you know what to look for. This will save you from having to look back and wonder what you ever saw in this man in the first place. All relationships are a growing, learning experience if we let them be, so don't beat yourself up over past mistakes, but take the lessons from them and start moving forward to your best relationship to date. Yes, it's much easier to look back and wonder where your head was, but it takes maturity to look at those past relationships and see them for what they were (and weren't) and your responsibility in them. It's always easy to point the finger at someone else and find something wrong with them, but it's difficult to look at yourself with clarity. Since you were the common denominator in all your past interactions, it's you who needs the insight of the role you played in getting to where you are. Once you understand how the dynamics played out, you are freer than you have ever been to have a different and better relationship that can endure the passage of time. You have just added a new item to your shopping list and become a better relationship shopper, because you have grown up and accepted responsibility for your childhood wounds.

2

Finding the Same Person Behind Different Masks

Analyzing Your Mate Selection and Finding That Common Thread

What's your modus operandi? We all have one, and you are now going to have the opportunity to see exactly what your mate-selection MO is and how it correlates directly to your parents. We'll begin to look at your parents as people, without the labels of Mom and Dad, and start identifying which voids you have been trying to fix through your romantic relationships. We'll also examine the similarities between your parents and the mates you choose.

You may feel you are stuck in a relationship rut, but once you are better informed, you can begin to make changes. In the past you might have chosen a partner who didn't ask much of you emotionally and didn't demand that you grow as a person within the relationship. This arrangement might have sounded easy at first, but if you eventually decided you wanted to grow and your partner couldn't handle intimacy, you found yourself stuck at a certain level and couldn't move beyond that. When you end up in this kind of dead-end relationship, it is most likely because you come from a family with a limited level of emotional intimacy.

On the other hand, maybe you choose partners who demand too much emotionally. You may feel smothered like my client Alyssa, who married a man from another country. He was new to the area, and she was his whole life. He would walk her out to the car when she left for the office in the morning, and he would run out the front door when she returned from work so he could open the car door for her. It was a little much since Alyssa had been independent for so long and didn't want, need, or enjoy the nonstop attention. She had the feeling of being under constant surveillance, just as she had been with her mother, who was always meddling in her life. Choosing that same type of person as her partner is similar to what most of us do, although maybe not to this degree or in such an obvious way.

You thought you had gotten away from childhood, but instead you find you've simply replaced one player for another and recreated exactly what you were trying so hard to get away from. It just isn't fair. But then life isn't fair, and the earlier we learn that, the better off we are. We can want a great relationship and do our absolute best to get one, but until our past is cleared up, we keep getting pulled back into it, fair or not. It isn't until we accept the unfairness and move forward that we can make changes in our lives.

Most of us are usually too blind to see the common thread and that we pick a mate who has the same behaviors or plays the same role as a parent. We see the role our mother and father played in their relationship with each other and also how they dealt with us. We choose this dynamic again not because we really want to repeat it, but because subconsciously it is a known quantity, we feel secure, and we know what to expect from those given roles. There won't be any big surprises in store for us and life can continue as always.

ANN:
MATERIAL GIFTS
DON'T REPLACE DAD'S
LACK OF ATTENTION

Ann was a well-respected doctor in her field and led a busy life. What she had trouble with was maintaining a relationship. She was devoted to her patients, but when she had a man in her life she wanted him there 24/7. She expected him to send flowers or give her gifts on a regular basis, and if he didn't, she would complain that he didn't care enough. If he complied with her requests, she upped the ante and wanted more.

As a little girl, Ann rarely saw her adored father. He enjoyed the frequent traveling he had to do for his profession and would bring her little gifts when he returned. She was always happy to see him and the presents he brought her, but it was a small substitute for having him there for her on a daily basis. Since material signs were all she had from him, she thought that gifts meant love and carried that idea into her adult relationships.

She kept choosing men who would give her gifts, not realizing that it wasn't the presents she really wanted, but more of their time. To Ann, it made sense to choose men who would give her gifts, because receiving them made her feel good again as an adult. The problem was that the men she selected couldn't give more of themselves, just as her dad couldn't. Things were all they had to give. She couldn't figure out why the men in her life never got closer and the closeness she so longed for remained only a hope and desire. She was unconscious of playing out the same role that she had with her father and thought she was really working toward intimacy with her latest love. But instead of pursuing real intimacy, she was trying—unwillingly and unsuccessfully—to heal her past.

Recognizing Your Love Fantasies

We all have absorbed different ideas of what love is and what it isn't. We can look at another couple and wonder what they see in each other, yet they may be looking back at us and wondering the same thing. This can be explained by examining the messages and wounds we have picked up from our families; everything we have absorbed is unique to our own upbringing, which is why we accept or fight about something that another person wouldn't give two cents about.

If you have an issue with punctuality and your honey is always late, you might make a big deal out of it, whereas someone else would simply shrug it off. One person might value punctuality because being on time shows them they are important and their feelings count. Someone who simply doesn't care if their loved one is late most likely gets the feeling of being special in some other way. We all want to feel special. The difference is in the way we feel it based on past programming and the fantasies we bring from childhood.

Take a look at these love fantasies, and see if any of them ring true for you:

- We have sexual chemistry, so we must be in love.
- Creating relationship drama means he cares.
- A relationship should always be calm.
- There should *never* be arguments.
- He loves me, so I should love him back.
- We're the same religion, race, nationality, or social standing, so that means we're compatible.
- We've been married forever, so we have to stick it out the rest of the way.
- Problems should be ignored for the good of a relationship.
- Falling in love should feel like getting hit with a ton of bricks.
- I'm comfortable with this man, so that must mean I love him.
- My family likes him, so he must be The One.
- He needs me to make his life better, and that's love.
- I don't feel "in love," but he's so nice to me, it must be.
- He's nothing like my parents, so I've made a good choice.
- It's the best relationship I've had so far, so it must be right.

Not one of these fantasies is about real love, yet many people believe them to be true or get wrapped up in them and proceed accordingly. In all of them, the thinking can be traced back to the way Mom and Dad dealt with the world in general and us in particular and the messages we picked up from them.

Suzanne: Living in a Soap Opera

Suzanne had been dating Ryan for seven years. Neither of them wanted marriage at this point as they really didn't get along that well, but they had a bond that they couldn't seem to break. At one point, Suzanne was pushing for marriage, but Ryan wasn't ready; then it would switch, and Ryan would want to be married, but Suzanne wasn't ready. They never seemed to be on the same page with this issue, so they just continued with what they had.

There was always drama in their relationship, often showing up as telephone calls ending in fights that went on until the wee hours of the morning. They would both be exhausted for work the next day, but that didn't stop them from continuing this pattern repeatedly. They took many vacations together and had fun, but sooner or later one would accuse the other of flirting with someone, and the arguing would start anew. During a cruise to the Caribbean, Suzanne became so angry that she threw a glass of wine in Ryan's face. Ryan stormed off to their cabin, but Suzanne followed and they made up—for the time being, anyway.

They had both come from families where emotions were kept under lock and key, not to be displayed, so in a certain way their acting out was exciting to them and meant that the other person really cared about them. Their fantasy was that if the other was expressing any feelings at all, it must be love. They eventually broke up, which took many months, and are now with new partners. In their current relationships, however, there is no emotion involved and they are really just arrangements. Suzanne and Ryan have gone from one extreme to the other, now thinking that maybe love means relationships run smoothly at all times. If they can get out of their romantic fantasies, they can work toward finding healthy relationships based on reality.

Check to see if you are operating under a relationship fantasy that isn't really meeting your needs. It may be dull or full of drama, but if it isn't bringing you what you want on a deep level, then it isn't the one for you. Instead, your fantasy is nestled in the past, which isn't going to get fixed by engaging in unhealthy relationship dynamics.

The Case of the Missing Parts

In order to take responsibility for your mate-selection incompatibilities in the past, you need to identify clearly what you have been seeking in relationships. Be honest as you think about the following statements, and you will begin to see a pattern emerge. Read each statement and rank yourself on a scale of one to ten, with one meaning the statement doesn't apply to you and ten meaning it describes you perfectly.

1. I choose partners who are below me in professional status, intelligence, or financial means.
2. I pick partners who are above me in those same areas.
3. I attract those who need me, and I take care of them.

4. I am never satisfied with whomever I choose for very long.
5. I expect my partner to be perfect.
6. I have accepted a going-nowhere relationship because I feel safe there.
7. My partner is nice but without a lot of substance.
8. I have difficulty living up to my partner's expectations.
9. I have to give up parts of myself in order to keep the relationship I have.
10. My partner and I have too many fights.
11. I get involved with people who want to take care of me.
12. If my partner would just see that I'm right, we'd be happy.
13. My relationship isn't the best, but it's the best I can expect.
14. I need to be in charge of my relationship.
15. I excuse too many of my partner's behaviors.

Any score of five or more means you may be facing one of the missing parts that is haunting you in relationshipland. If you scored highest on statements 2, 6, 9, or 13, you are missing a sense of self-worth. If you scored highest on 3, 7, or 11, you didn't get enough nurturing and are seeking that in adulthood. If you scored highest on 1, 10, 12, or 14, power and control were important in your family and you are perpetuating that behavior. If you scored highest on 4, 5, 8, or 15, you were not given a sense of self; life was all about your parents and not enough about you. Once you figure out what you've been missing, you will see what you've been trying to find.

Chances are you're beginning to realize that it's not by accident that you choose your partners but rather as a way to fill up holes that are left over from the past. It's not your fault that you've made these choices—it's practically predetermined. It's almost as if it were written in the stars during your childhood and affects you from there on. Take heart knowing that your predetermined path can be altered. Once you learn to see the parent trap for what it is, you can change your take on life and relationships and make them into something great. It's all in your very capable hands.

MARGARET: FINDING HER DAD IN A DIFFERENT GUISE AGAIN AND AGAIN

Margaret's dad was an alcoholic, one of those quiet types who drank when he got home from work until he passed out, only to get up the next day and repeat the pattern. He was a gentle soul without a mean bone in him, but he was totally unavailable to Margaret or anyone else in the family for talks, nurturing, advice, or direction.

Margaret met the first "love of her life" and married him. Ten years later, when he wanted a divorce, she was devastated. She was unaware that they didn't have a close relationship because she hadn't experienced one with either her mom or her dad, so she didn't know what it was like. She only knew that she hadn't married an alcoholic, so she was certainly doing it differently than her parents. She wasn't going to "marry Dad," that's for sure. She didn't like the feeling of always coming second to the booze, so she always looked for men who hardly touched a drop of alcohol, and drugs were so far out of the equation that they didn't even exist in her world.

The second "love of her life" came along and she married him too, but she started realizing he was even less emotionally available than her first husband had been. At least with her first husband, they did things together, but this one wasn't much interested in togetherness, which only showed up after the marriage. She was in a quandary, wondering where she had gone wrong.

Neither men were drinkers nor did they have any major flaws to the casual eye. But stripping away what they looked like on the outside, they were her dad all over again, with no emotional availability to invest in a relationship. They just did it without the liquor. Margaret was operating out of a few relationship fantasies. She was comfortable in relationships with these men and thought that meant love. Also, these relationships were calm, but that was because the men weren't invested emotionally. She just knew that she had chosen someone unlike her parents, so that was supposed to make everything run smoothly and love was going to grow and flourish.

When Margaret realized what she had been doing, she was flabbergasted. She never thought she was repeating the same dynamics of long ago. She had chosen men who were far from being substance abusers, and she thought she had done it right. With some insight, however, she saw that she had chosen men who were like her father. Subconsciously she had believed that if she could be emotionally involved with these men, she would feel like she really mattered and her dad had been wrong in choosing alcohol over her. Of course, these men were incapable of such involvement, so all she got was a comfortable relationship, or at least one she knew about, but with no substance and no fulfillment of her deeper needs.

Sometimes the tie-in to past experiences is subtle, so you have to look below the surface at what isn't outwardly apparent. When you do see the connection, it all becomes crystal clear and answers many of the questions regarding the reasons you chose one person over the other and why you thought "he" was the perfect person for you. Let's make you even wiser by investigating what you were exposed to growing up.

Who Are These People Who Raised Me?

Take this quiz and find out what you know and what you don't about your parents. Looking at the faces they presented to the world will help define the hidden messages you got from them.

1. Was Dad really happy under that solemn face? Was there a depressive quality to him, or was he the quiet

type who could still see humor in life? What about Mom?

2. Did Mom harbor a secret resentment because she didn't live out her dreams by becoming a Broadway dancer or a CEO, becoming a wife and mother instead? Did Dad resent having to raise a family instead of following his dreams?

3. Did Mom and Dad see the glass as half-full or half-empty?

4. Do their professions fit with who they really are?

5. Do you think they are or were happily married?

6. Why do you think they got married in the first place?

7. Did they take a hands-on or hands-off approach with you?

8. Do you know anything about their previous relationships?

9. Were they there in body only, not giving you much direction or affection? Where do you think they would have rather been?

10. What are their relationships with their siblings like?

11. Did they give you space to be who you were?

12. Were they angry?

13. Were finances handled wisely by both of them?

14. Who did the most talking?

15. What were their childhoods like? Did they have loving parents, or did their upbringing leave something to be desired?

16. Did they experience love and respect when they were growing up?

17. Were they supported in a kind and loving way?

Try to be as honest as you can with your answers. Examining the way you were raised and under what circumstances gives you a good idea of what type of person you seek out for romantic relationships. For example, if life was all about your parents and you were just along for the ride, you might choose someone who appears to feel that you are important to him, but if you look closer, you will see that he is satisfying his own needs and life is again all about him. He might try to keep you happy because he wants to come across as the nicest guy around. That's how he gets his kudos, and it doesn't really have anything to do with how much he cares about you in the long run, even though it sure looked like it at the beginning. This was a familiar model for you, so it felt comfortable. Without any guidelines as to how a more intimate relationship looks or operates, you became stuck with the same one you saw growing up.

If you idolize your father and have put him on a pedestal, try to make him more human as you are filling out the questionnaire. We *all* have our issues; no one is free from them, even if "The Brady Bunch" portrayed the family as being perfect. A TV show is one thing, real life is another. I don't mean you have to make him out to be a bad guy, but try to see exactly what the issues were he had to deal with. I had a client who thought her father was perfect until one day she suddenly had an epiphany. We had been working on her issues for some time when she realized that because her father came from a home where both of his parents died young he probably dealt with abandonment issues. She was then free to see him as simply another human trying to do the best he could. Set yourself free and see your parents as having some blemishes here and there just like the rest of us.

Sarah Jane: Abandonment Leads to Smothering

Sarah Jane had a hard time growing up. Her parents divorced when she was ten, and her mother wanted to move to another state. Her father fought for her, and her mother decided to appease him by leaving Sarah Jane and coming back for her later. She thought he would have cooled down by then, and they could have a smoother time raising Sarah Jane. Of course, Sarah Jane wasn't given a choice in the matter and felt abandoned by her mom, which for all intents and purposes, she was.

When her mom did return, her parents decided to share Sarah Jane and have her stay a week at one house and a week at the other. Her dad had remarried and wanted some time alone with his new wife; Sarah Jane didn't much like her new stepmom. Then her mom met and married a man who was nice enough, but emotionally unavailable and had difficulty connecting with other people, so her mom had to give him all kinds of love and attention to try to rescue him. Sarah Jane was still abandoned even though both parents were present and trying to make it all work. Although the first abandonment had been a physical one by her mom, the second was emotional by both parents.

In her late teens, she met a young man she thought was wonderful. They started dating, and soon they were spending all their time together. Sarah Jane felt like she had hit the jackpot, because here was someone who was going to give her the attention she so sorely

lacked from her parents. As time went on, her boyfriend started feeling smothered as Sarah Jane wanted to
spend every possible moment with him. He suggested
she join a gym or take a class one evening a week, but
she replied that she would miss him too much to be
away that long. The more she pushed to be together,
the more he pulled away.

What he was hinting at was that he needed some
space, and if she could give that to him, they would
be much happier together. She couldn't see what was
going on because she was so scared of being neglected
again that she came on too strong and too needy. She
was holding on for dear life, trying to heal the wounds
of her earlier rejection. As he became more and more
emotionally distant, she came on even stronger, and it
wasn't long before he broke up with her.

Sarah Jane just had to be in a relationship to prove
her worth, so she went right out and got another boyfriend. Because she's never been able to identify the
detachment relationship pattern set by her parents, she's
doomed to repeat the same mistake of being ruled by
her neediness over and over.

Connecting the Dots: Linking Who Your Parents Are to Who You're Attracted To

Understanding how your choices mimic the past is a necessary step in eliminating patterns that emerge in your mate
selection. Have you ever wondered about the following?

- Why you gravitate to the same type of person over and over
- Why you hook up with people who make you feel uncomfortable in some way
- Why you feel something is always missing in your relationships
- Why you remained in a relationship long after it was really over
- Why you don't like your partner better than you do
- Why you can never find the "right" person
- Why your relationships never match your ideal
- Why you "settle for" a certain person
- Why you are never happy for long in your relationships
- Why you go from relationship to relationship

If so, you will now be able to see why. It's all part and parcel of being caught up in the parent trap and bringing that forward into your adult life.

What Makes Your Heart Go Pitter-Pat?

Write down the names of your most significant past partners. Under each name, list his traits, both good and bad. What qualities and ways of relating to the world did these men exhibit? Here are a few examples of descriptions you might use:

Abusive
Accountable
Angry
Boring
Close-minded
Deceptive

Dependent
Generous
Happy-go-lucky
Humorous
Immature
Insincere
Looking to be rescued
Low sex drive
Manipulative
Mature
Nonexpressive
No-nonsense
Open-minded
Passive
Pleaser
Practical
Sarcastic
Self-doubting
Sincere
Stable
Still attached to parents or ex
Timid
Truthful
Unfaithful
Unreliable
Victim
Without passion

Now take a close look at the traits that your previous partners have in common, especially the negative traits. Think about what you didn't like about the men on your list and what didn't work for you in building a fully committed, long-term relationship.

The Whole Package

You've focused on the negative traits of the men in your life, but they had positive traits also, so don't get too down on yourself. You certainly didn't get involved with someone because he had nothing but negative traits, but to be a savvy shopper, you have to look at the *whole package*. We all have a smattering of both strengths and weaknesses, and it's up to you to decide which way the scale balances and what really works for you. Do his strengths outweigh his flaws, or are you using selective thinking and downplaying his weaknesses? This is very important, but most people don't take it seriously. You might mouth the words, but at the start of a relationship when you think you can't live without the other person and your relationship is "special," you may have a tendency to deny or overlook those negative parts that will eventually show up to haunt you down the road.

You might be able to look at a friend and see exactly what she is not seeing in her beau, but you put blinders on when it comes to your own situation. The good parts to his character may be so good that you can't see that other not-so-good characteristics are present as well. Love certainly can be blind at the beginning of a relationship, but that's just when you need the clearest twenty-twenty sight there is.

CARRIE:
TRYING TO OUTRUN
DAD'S SERIOUSNESS

There wasn't a lot of humor in Carrie's home when she was growing up. Life with her parents always had a depressive undercurrent running through it. Nothing was ever said about what was wrong, but the feeling was always there, dulling everything that happened. There was never any talk about feelings either, so Carrie felt isolated and alone in her own family. While her mom tried to be light and outgoing, it didn't come across as genuine. Part of the reason was because her dad was a strict, no-nonsense type of man, so her mother couldn't get too far away from the cloud that hung over the family.

When Carrie began to date, she always looked for men who had a great sense of humor and were on the unconventional side. Her first major boyfriend in high school was popular and funny and had lots of friends. They were always laughing and having a great time. Carrie thought she had met the man of her dreams, as he was always willing to try new things and could see the humorous side of everything.

They got engaged in college, but then Carrie began to see that his life was all about him. He cared for her, but he always came first with no understanding of what she might be feeling. She met someone else and broke off the engagement. He eventually became an alcoholic, moved from job to job, and showed up on the unemployed list more often than not. Someone who had looked like a happy-go-lucky guy in high school turned out to have some major issues, one of them being that depression she was trying to get away from.

In the ensuing years, she married twice and then dated lots of different men. She always looked for that humor aspect, not realizing there wasn't a lot of depth to these men and that they also had some major issues.

It simply felt to her that if they could laugh together, their relationship would be nothing like her parents'.

With help, she eventually saw what she was doing. Now when she meets someone who makes her laugh and that click happens, she knows to look beyond it and see what else the package contains. She is getting to be a better and better shopper in the men department, and one of these days, she will meet someone who has all the parts of the package, because now she knows to look underneath the surface and that initial draw of laughter.

To gain confidence in your relationships all you need is some clarification as to why you did it a certain way in the past. Once you learn this you are able to look at your present and future relationships in a whole new and different way. It's exciting when you think of the time, energy, and hurt you are going to not invest in any longer, but instead bring in the happiness that has been out of your reach until now.

Mom and Dad's Dynamics

When you can step back and look at the dynamics between your parents, you will gain even more information about what made you the person you are today. You might see that you're recreating your mom or dad's role in their marriage in your own relationships, or you might see that you're trying to rescue one of your parents or make life better for one of them because they had it so rough.

My guess is you don't want to do that; you would rather have your very own relationship. I agree with you wholeheartedly—repeating someone else's role doesn't allow you to be who you are and live life to its fullest based on your personal needs. You are only going to find true happiness in relationships when you let go of the past and live completely in the present as the person you were meant to be.

So, to this end, you need to be your own therapist for a moment and complete the following worksheet about what you saw growing up with your parents and your more mature views of them now that you are an adult.

Mom and Dad Under the Microscope

1. Dad showed his anger.   Yes   No

   He got mad at Mom about _____.

   He showed it by _____.

2. Dad showed affection.   Yes   No

   He liked it when Mom _____.

   He showed it by _____.

3. Dad got frustrated.   Yes   No

   He got frustrated when Mom _____.

   He showed it by _____.

4. He withdrew into his shell.   Yes   No

   This was prompted by _____.

When it happened, how did he treat Mom? _____

_____ .

He showed that displeasure by _____

_____ .

5. He showed Mom his displeasure.   Yes   No

6. He communicated his feelings.   Yes   No

The positive feelings he showed were _____

_____ .

The negative feelings he showed were _____

_____ .

7. He was kind to Mom.   Yes   No

He showed his kindness by_____ .

8. He manipulated Mom.   Yes   No

He liked to be in control by_____ .

9. He was abusive to Mom.   Yes   No

He did this as often as_____ .

He did this by _____ .

10. He gave Mom anything she wanted.   Yes   No

To do this, he had to sacrifice_____.

He did it with an attitude of_____.

11. He fought with Mom.   Yes   No

His method of fighting was _____.

How often did he "win"? _____.

12. He didn't like it when Mom did certain things like

_____.

He communicated it by_____.

13. He respected Mom and valued her opinion. Yes   No

He showed this by _____.

He liked Mom because _____.

14. He tried to make life nice for Mom.   Yes   No

He did this by _____.

Why did he do this? _____.

Now answer these same questions about your mother:

1. Mom showed her anger.   Yes   No

She got mad at Dad about _____.

She showed her anger by _____.

2. Mom showed affection.   Yes   No

She liked it when Dad _____.

She showed it by _____.

3. Mom got frustrated.   Yes   No

She got frustrated when Dad _____.

She showed it by _____.

4. She withdrew into her shell.   Yes   No

This was prompted by _____.

When it happened, how did she treat Dad? _____

_____.

5. She showed Dad her displeasure.   Yes   No

6. She communicated her feelings.   Yes   No

The positive feelings she showed were _____

_____.

The negative feelings she showed were _____

_____.

7. She was kind to Dad.   Yes   No

She showed her kindness by_____.

8. She manipulated Dad.   Yes   No

She liked to be in control by_____.

9. She was abusive to Dad.   Yes   No

She did this by_____.

She did this as often as _____.

10. She gave Dad anything he wanted.   Yes   No

To do this, she had to sacrifice_____.

She did it with an attitude of_____.

11. She fought with Dad.   Yes   No

Her method of fighting was _____.

How often did she "win"? _____.

She communicated it by _____.

12. She didn't like it when Dad did certain things like

_____ .

She showed that displeasure by _____

_____ .

13. She respected Dad and valued his opinion.   Yes   No

She showed this by _____ .

She liked Dad because _____ .

14. She tried to make life nice for Dad.   Yes   No

She did this by _____ .

Why did she do this? _____ .

Now let's look at what you discerned from their relationship. Your parents' relationship dynamic is part of the positive and negative baggage you bring into all of your relationships. Complete the following sentences to see what you've been carrying around inside your suitcase. List the good and the bad. For example, you might generally think men are intelligent but lazy, or insensitive but fun.

Based on what I saw, I believe my parents were (happy,

unhappy) _____ .

The message I picked up about relationships was

_____ .

I think men are _____ .

I think women are _____ .

I want my partner to be_____ .

In a partnership, I think I should be_____ .

I think relationships should have these qualities:

_____ .

As you look at your answers, see what beliefs you have adopted in your adult partnerships. If you believe that relationships are necessary and you have to stay in them no matter what, have you done that to your detriment when it would have been better for you to say good-bye and move on?

As each day passes, try to set a clearer relationship goal for yourself. Ask yourself what you want in a relationship. Begin to realize that you don't have to reenact your parents' relationship dynamics.

The Picture Emerges

Take a minute to look back at the examples and insights you've developed so far in this chapter. You are ready to take the next step: drawing lines between Mom, Dad, and your mate and seeing how messages you absorbed in your childhood are playing out in today's relationships. You can begin the process of linking the past to your present choices of desirable mates.

With the checklist "Who Are These People Who Raised Me?" you had the opportunity to identify and examine the positive and negative qualities of each parent along with their personalities, characters, and temperaments. You also have lists with the traits of your mom, your dad, their relationship with each other, and the partners you have chosen in life. Maybe you can see that your mom was controlling, humorless, demanding, and critical and that her life was very structured. Perhaps on your dad's list, you wrote that he was passive, unexciting, uninvolved, domineering, or abusive. In your evaluation of their relationship, you might have seen them as serious, manipulative, and/or withdrawn. Next, you can look at the qualities you listed for your past partners and find the common ones. Does one common trait start to stand out above all?

The next crucial step is to compare all the lists to each other. You should see some similarities between Mom or Dad—or Mom *and* Dad—and the people you have selected in the romance department. The likenesses are there; there is no way for them not to be. They may simply be hidden from your sight until you get the hang of looking at them differently. If your father was noncommittal, your mates might be unresponsive emotionally. If your mother was depressed, you might find that you pick men who have no passion in life. Always look for the emotional availability of each of your parents and see how this shows up with your honey, past or present. If Mom was critical, did you choose a man who allowed you to criticize him so, in that respect, you married your dad?

The Domino Effect of the Parent Trap

The following table gives examples of how your past has influenced your adult life and why your selection process for choosing a mate is what it is. These are common examples of what women try to re-create and heal with their relationships.

Remember when looking at this list that this is what you picked up as a child. If you were exposed to these situations as an adult, you would take in an entirely different message because you would be able to reason it out. According to child psychology experts, these messages are picked up by the time a child is eight years old, so don't be too hard on yourself and think you should have known better. If you could have, you would have.

Understanding Hidden Messages

Past Situation	Hidden Message	Resulting Partner Selection
Dad said one thing and did another.	Men are irresponsible and can't be trusted.	I choose men who will disappoint me in both small and large ways.
Mom didn't give me physical or emotional love.	There is something wrong with me, and I am not lovable.	I choose partners who are emotionally unavailable and unable to give me what I want.

(continued)

Understanding Hidden Messages *(continued)*

Past Situation	Hidden Message	Resulting Partner Selection
Dad had rages.	I have to hide my feelings so I don't upset anyone.	I choose partners who have anger issues or ones who won't listen to my feelings.
Mom always criticized my weight problem.	There is something wrong with me, and I'm not okay the way I am.	I try to please men with my humor or niceness or friendship, but they never let me feel like I measure up to their ideal.
Dad was mean to Mom.	I have to be good at all costs so the anger isn't directed at me.	I pick partners who are emotionally absent and only interested in what's good for them and how their own needs can be met.
I had to take care of my siblings because my parents didn't want to.	My merit is based on taking care of others.	I choose mates who are immature and need mothering.
I felt sorry for Mom.	I am only worthy if I save others.	I get hooked up with men I can rescue.
My dad had affairs.	Men can't be trusted.	I find men who are untrustworthy, still emotionally holding on to a past love, or who have some sort of addictive personality.
My dad sexually molested me, so I'm "bad."	I am only safe when someone has all the power.	I find men who either control the relationship or men who let me control it so I can feel safe.
Mom died when I was very young.	People I love leave me.	I try to please men so they will stay with me.

Past Situation	Hidden Message	Resulting Partner Selection
My dad was an alcoholic.	I don't matter unless I can make someone else's life better.	I attract men who I think I can fix and gain their undying love and appreciation.
Dad was never affectionate with Mom.	I don't deserve all that a relationship can offer.	I choose men who have a low sex drive and don't desire me.
The outside world was more important to my parents than I was.	I'm not as good as everything else in someone's life.	I can't fully commit to the men I choose nor can they commit to me.
My parents never fought in front of me or let me see they were having problems and then all of a sudden they divorced.	I'm not important enough to be told the truth.	I choose men I can't trust because I don't expect them to ever tell me the truth.
Mom was a perfectionist and everything I did could have been better.	I can never measure up to someone's expectations.	I choose men who have major issues so that I can feel superior to them.
Mom and Dad struggled financially, and life was always hard.	I have to know I'm "better than" someone else and have him dependent on me to feel safe.	I choose men who have less than I do.

Breaking the Tie That Binds

You've done some major homework in this chapter and have hopefully gleaned a lot of good information as to the whys and hows of your relationships. This is a major step in break-ing the invisible link you have with your parents. No one escapes; it's just a matter of degree. You can have so many links that you can't even count them all, or you can have just a few, but they all count and affect your relationships. Once you see the connections, you are able to start moving in a healthy direction.

There may even be some aspects of your parents' relation-ship that you would like to emulate but haven't been able to put into practice. If this is the case, think about what those aspects are and make a list of those qualities. Perhaps your parents were good together at finances and taught you how to spend and how to save, but you haven't gotten it right yet and have lots of credit card debt with little or no savings. If you want to follow their teachings you will want to make yourself a goal to pursue a more balanced financial picture. If they shared the housework and you and your partner don't, then hold up, in your mind, what that looks like and begin discussions toward that end. Often, there are aspects of your parents' relationship that are positive, so don't get in the mindset that they had an all bad one.

It's as if there is an undetectable rubber band between you and your past that keeps snapping you back to your old beliefs and behaviors. This rubber band never gets old and never breaks; it stays as strong as the first day it was put in place. The only thing that loosens its elasticity is the under-standing of how it got there in the first place and your desire to be out of its grasp. Once you start working on this, the band starts to wear down; the more work you do and the more insight you have, the thinner it gets. Loosening its hold is within your control. You are well on your way to making that previously undetected rubber band weaker. And though it might never break completely, the times it shows up get further and further apart and become less and less impacting. You will notice when it's there, recognize that it's behavior from the past, and then be able to move away from it in a short amount of time.

In the next chapter, you will look at how your past experiences evolved into coping mechanisms for your adult relationships. This next step continues to make that band get looser and looser as you keep getting smarter and smarter.

3

How You Escape the Lions and Tigers and Bears in Relationships

Recognizing Your Coping Mechanisms in Relationships

Now that you've identified the type of person to whom you've been attracted and why that's the case, the picture has become clearer as to the similarities between Mom and/or Dad and your love interests. You have that in your shopping cart so now you are going to move to the next aisle and begin looking at how you relate in relationships based on the fears you brought forth from childhood—again, what you are attracted to that reminds you of your parents.

We all have fears, so don't think you are some kind of strange duck who's beyond saving—au contraire. It's all about knowing how prevalent these fears are in your life and how much they interfere with your having the best possible life you can. This chapter will show you how to identify when you are functioning as a grown-up person and when you have become a little girl again. This insight allows you to understand the fears you and the men in your life are operating under. A word of caution here: Be careful not to fall into the trap of accepting poor behavior as OK simply because you understand the reasons behind it. You never have to accept behavior that doesn't respect you or your relationship.

Many, many people do just that and overlook behaviors that are unproductive. My client Joanna understood that her husband's mother suffocated him emotionally throughout his childhood and that the woman still tried to be overinvolved in his adult life. Joanna could see it firsthand. During their marriage, she had excused his workaholic behavior because she was afraid that if she hassled him about it, he would see it as a repeat of his mother's way of relating and start to ignore her just as he tried to do with his mother. Still, Joanna came to me because she was unhappy that they were growing further apart and that her husband's time away from the family was increasing. She had thought her tolerance of his behavior would give him space and help him heal his past; he would realize she wasn't his mother, trust her, and spend more time with her. Her plan wasn't working out the way she'd thought it would, and she didn't know if she could go on this way with the two of them growing even more distant and her feeling more abandoned.

In this example, Joanna's husband's fear of being suffocated and her fear of abandonment were ruining their marriage. There are ramifications of acting out your fears, so be aware of how they are interfering in your relationship. Once you recognize when a certain fear is showing up, you can begin to understand it and start working on changing your behavior. Unlike Joanna, you shouldn't excuse your partner's fears. Instead, try pointing out—in a positive, caring way—to yourself and even your mate what you think is popping up from the past. The more knowledge you have, the more you can bring that awareness to the fore and the smoother your relationships can go. It takes two people to do this, and if you are both willing to communicate, you are on your way to creating more harmony for both of you.

When you're looking at your fears, appreciate the fact that they are learned instincts. We weren't born immediately knowing how to speak French, English, or Italian; it was something we were taught and had to learn in order to communicate with everyone around us. Just as we learned a particular language, we also learned how to interact with the people in our world and how to deal with different situations. These were the coping mechanisms that we learned in our first years on earth and are a direct result of how our parents either did or didn't meet our needs. These behaviors are defenses against insufficient nurturing, over which we had no control.

The four coping mechanisms we will discuss in this chapter are extreme examples; most people are going to fall someplace in the middle. For most of us, fears creep up temporarily and then recede without affecting our lives or relationships, but for others, the presence of fear is a way of life. They live with their fears always just below the surface of their consciousness. You need to look carefully at your life to determine how much your fears influence you.

Fear creates a ripple effect. If you fear loss in your relationships, you will also see that crop up in your work, your friendships, and even with your children, so look at all areas of your life and see if you notice a common theme. If we create drama in our lives, withdraw into a shell, detach, either shun or crave affection, want to be attached to our partner at the hip, or react to criticism either by yelling or crying or running away, we are using our traditional ways of coping with our feelings of not feeling safe. Mom and Dad were the instigators of this behavior, and we continue to react to our partners in the same way we reacted to our parents. It's a never-ending cycle of acting like an adult and then retreating into childish behavior when we perceive that our security is threatened; then it's back to adulthood until the next time we feel vulnerable. We can't break free until we understand what our patterns are and where they come from.

Melanie: Marrying Mom the Adversary

Melanie grew up with a mother who always criticized her. Her mother would yell and sometimes even physically push her around. Melanie discovered at a young age that she had no power in relationships and therefore didn't believe she was worth much. She was a sensitive girl and felt that if she showed her sensitive side, she would be exposed to more hurt from her mother, so she coped by protecting the part of her that feared abandonment

In her teenage years, she found that she was strong enough to start yelling back and that it felt good to give her mom a push to the shoulder here and there. She became one of the players and had as much control as her mother. She carried this combative attitude into her adult relationships, not realizing she was now grown up and had options about who she partnered with and how that partnership operated. She didn't understand that until much later in life.

Her father had been an easygoing man who seemed to be OK with the treatment Melanie received at her mom's hands—at least, he certainly didn't stop it. Melanie had no respect for him because, to all intents and purposes, he had abandoned her, and it felt like he had thrown her to the wolves, with the leader of the pack being her mom.

Because she identified with her mother, Melanie was destined to marry a strong-willed man who would engage with her in exactly the same way her mom had. She and her husband had shouting matches that at times became physical. Once the police were called by a concerned neighbor, as they lived in an upscale neighborhood where that type of thing wasn't supposed to happen. She eventually got caught up in drugs, and her husband divorced her, taking their daughter with him.

Melanie had effectively married her mother (because of all the turmoil), but it also felt like she had married her father (because of her husband and child's eventual abandonment). Her fear of abandonment had come true, and she was stuck right back in childhood.

Even when we see that it's not productive to behave the way we do, we stick to it because it's what we're comfortable with—it's the game we know how to play. To this end, we choose men who recreate what we knew and experienced in childhood. Or we choose the opposite and think we've gotten away from Mom or Dad. But we can't truly escape our fears until we face them head-on.

The Four Basic Fears

To counter fears from childhood, you come up with coping skills that help you feel fairly safe and not totally at your fear's mercy. Without these skills, you would never venture into a relationship of any kind. It would be too painful and leave you too exposed. Some of the more extreme cases you read about in the news are of people who were not able to develop the coping skills they needed to survive in life so they went off the deep end in some way.

The vast majority of us, however, do develop these skills. Four basic fears surface over and over for all of us. There are also common coping skills that correspond to each of these fears. Look over the following list, then we'll discuss each one in more depth.

• **Please be consistent with me.** This is the *fear of abandonment*, resulting from a parent's "come here/go away" messages. If you had a parent who was emotionally inconsistent and unpredictable, you either developed a clinging response or emotionally keep your distance to feel safe. You also may develop an unstable love/hate relationship with your partners.

• **Please don't smother me.** This is the *fear of being absorbed*, resulting from a parent's overprotectiveness. If your parents were domineering or overinvolved in your life, you will fear getting trapped in a relationship or will succumb to one just because it's there. You will also have trouble getting in touch with your feelings.

• **Please approve of me.** The *fear of rejection* arises if your parents were consistently giving you "go away" messages. You will detach from any person with whom you are in a relationship to avoid being dependent, or you will constantly seek approval and acceptance from a partner, becoming whatever others want you to be and having little sense of self. You may view yourself as seriously flawed.

• **Please don't leave me.** The *fear of loss* results from a parent's "don't be dependent" messages because that parent wasn't interested in meeting your needs and insisted that you separate more than you were ready for. The issue for you as an adult is to remain attached at all costs or to avoid relationships because you believe you are never going to have your needs met. You have difficulty trusting others.

Does any one fear in particular jump out at you, or does fear run more silently in your life? Sometimes it's apparent, and other times it's very subtle and difficult to detect. Let's take them one by one so you can see which ones you have been grappling with and to what degree. Remember you can look at yourself as well as those people who are important in your life. You can come to a better understanding of people's motivations in general once you have insight into their fears.

Fear of Abandonment

Some parents treat their children with a come here/go away attitude. Sometimes they want the child close and give her a great deal of love and affection; at other times, they don't want to be bothered. The child loves the come-here times as it makes her feel worthwhile. Pleasing a parent is a crucial validation that helps children develop a sense of self-worth in their younger years.

The come-here message feels good, but if a parent then turns around and doesn't have any time or interest in the child, it is very confusing. A parent can give the go-away message by saying coldly, "I'm too busy right now," "Go play by yourself and don't bother me," "I don't feel well," "You are being naughty, and I don't want to be around you," "I have to be gone every weekend this month, and I'm leaving you with your stepdad even though I know you don't like him," or similar words.

While these words are not necessarily damaging in themselves—all parents use some version of them at times—it's the emotional connection that is important here. If these statements are phrased with compassion for the child, that's one thing; but if they are said in a dismissive, unfeeling manner, that's another. If a parent is all warm and fuzzy one time and cold and distant the next, and that cycle is repeated time after time, the child develops a strategy to cope with this behavior so she can feel somewhat safe in her environment. She may love her parent one minute and dislike him or her the next, depending on whether that parent is emotionally inviting the child to get close or giving the go-away message. You can see how confusing this can be to a child. As a consequence, love and dislike can become interwoven in your relationship with your loved ones.

THE COPING MECHANISMS. One coping mechanism for the fear of abandonment is for the child to cling to the parent in hopes that he or she will eventually meet her security needs. The child feels obsessed with getting her parent to pay attention to her so she can get the warm, loving feeling on a regular basis. She looks for any and all emotional connections she can get and doesn't want to miss out on any potentially loving interaction.

With the opposite coping mechanism, the child detaches. She decides it's not safe to want affection because she doesn't know if she's going to be deserted at a moment when she needs the connection the most. To her way of thinking, she's better off just avoiding the whole issue. She protects herself by convincing herself that she doesn't need anyone.

CAN YOU SEE YOURSELF HERE? Look at these statements and see if you identify with any of them.

- You don't feel safe in relationships and withhold your feelings from your partner.
- You simultaneously crave and push away affection.
- You are passive-aggressive.
- You believe you can't get your needs met.
- You find it hard to trust others.

Fear of Being Absorbed

Some parents hold on to their child for dear life, never wanting her to stray too far away. If the child attempts to be more independent, the parents do whatever they can to squelch any exploration of the world she tries on her own. These parents may be afraid of the world because they are unsure of themselves. They may have missed the connection to their own parents, so they seek it with their child. In this case, the child becomes a substitute for the love the parents missed out on in their own childhood.

The overprotective parent makes strict rules, has to know all of a child's comings and goings, and has to be involved in everything the child does. This type of parent might also push the limit on physical affection, always wanting a hug or a kiss, to sit with the child snuggled up on the couch, or even to sleep with the child long after it's a normal and natural thing to do. This parent may also be overinvolved with the child's school or sports activities or her hobbies. The parent doesn't want, and therefore will not allow, a separation.

Physical closeness, involvement, and interest are all healthy to a certain degree. But when it goes beyond that line and becomes smothering, the child has to develop a coping mechanism to deal with her fear of being turned into either Mom or Dad without sufficient room for self-exploration.

THE COPING MECHANISMS. When fear of absorption occurs, a child has difficulty with self-image resulting in not being able to speak up about personal feelings and needs because that was not allowed. This child can put on a façade of not caring or trying to be the perfect child that the parent needs. Underneath that façade, of course, is a lot of pent-up anger and frustration.

Those who detach decide that there is no way their autonomy is going to be controlled by another, so they remain aloof and remote to protect themselves from too much involvement. It might be a lonely place, but it's all theirs, and no one else can take it away from them; they aren't available to be smothered. Although this reaction makes logical sense, they miss out on ever having a healthy connection to another person. They decided long ago that relationships aren't safe and have given up the opportunity to bond emotionally.

Individuals who outwardly comply with the burden of being smothered by a parent have decided it's easier to seem to accept the situation and go along with it, all the time inwardly building up more anger. In this case, the outer person and the inner person are two totally different individuals, and what you see isn't what you get if you scratch the surface.

CAN YOU SEE YOURSELF HERE? Look at these statements and see if you identify with any of them.

- You fear being taken over by someone else.
- You can't say no and be loved at the same time.
- You must maintain your personal freedom at all costs.
- You feel you have no personal identity.
- You have trouble getting in touch with your feelings.
- Being dependent is uncomfortable for you.

Fear of Rejection

A parent is supposed to be warm, loving, and kind, but there are parents who really aren't equipped to handle a child's emotional needs—not because they don't want to, but because they can't, based on what happened to them as children. These parents are always detached, cold, and emotionally unresponsive. They had to shut down their own emotional needs at an early age and bring that isolation into the parenting of their own children.

This is the parent you've heard at the store saying, "Stop crying this minute, or I'm going to spank you!" The child's needs have just been rejected, so she has to suck it up and swallow her needs or be hurt on a physical level. Or this is the father who tells his child in front of others, "Go play on the freeway," thinking this is funny; of course, to the child, it isn't funny at all. This parent can simply always be too busy or too tired or too sick to want much to do with the child. She is rejected in favor of the parent's needs, which always come first.

Fear of rejection operates in almost all of us to some degree, because parents can't be perfect. It's extremely difficult to always be there for children and meet all of their needs. Because all parents, just by nature of being human, make mistakes, you will inevitably experience some degree of this fear. But try to see if you are experiencing it to a low degree or a high one. It's the overwhelming fear of rejection that affects how we interact with others and interferes with our choices in relationships.

THE COPING MECHANISMS. The most common coping mechanism for someone who's terrified of rejection is to avoid close emotional contact with others. Since a parent shunned them, the only safe way to handle their fear is to not only give up on getting their needs met, but to deny to themselves that they have any needs in the first place. They operate under the principle that if a parent has rejected them, they will turn around and reject themselves, numbing their feelings.

They usually want an emotional contact with a parent, but because of their fear, reject that same parent. Now they have been rejected by a parent, have rejected their parent, and have rejected themselves. It's a going-nowhere situation fraught with self-denial and low self-esteem. In the end, they split off from anything that might bring them pleasure because they believe that a corresponding pain will come right along with it. This is slightly different from the emotional distance caused by the fear of being absorbed. The fear of rejection takes away from a person's outward show of self-confidence and the feeling of being safe in the world, whereas the fear of absorption results in a person who outwardly acts as if they don't need anyone. They are similar in that they both have repressed anger and they both feel alone in the world.

Other people who fear rejection crave acceptance to the extreme and will make themselves doormats for others in the hope that they won't be rejected again. They always want Mom and/or Dad's acceptance and will do whatever they have to throughout their lives to try to get it. They will do anything in their power to guarantee that a parent and other loved ones will like them and not emotionally desert them. They are so dependent on others that they don't have a separate sense of self; they instead become what they believe others want them to be.

CAN YOU SEE YOURSELF HERE? Look at these statements and see if you identify with any of them.

- You dislike too much togetherness.
- You fear physical rejection.
- You feel safe if you can hold on to someone.
- You are demanding of others.
- You think others are too emotional.
- You believe you have to conform to others' views to be lovable.

Fear of Loss

"Be a big girl and go play by yourself." "You are spending the night at Auntie Jane's whether you want to or not. You can handle it." "Don't bother me now, I'm busy." These are all statements from the parent who doesn't want to be bothered by a dependent child's needs. There are no "come here, go away" scenes as in the fear of abandonment, just "go away" messages. This parent is also simply "not there," whether physically or emotionally, especially when the child reaches out for help by trying to express her fears or needs. The parent expects this child to separate before she is ready to do so.

The fear of loss causes the child to feel insecure and overly dependent on this parent. She's afraid if she doesn't see Mom or Dad, that parent will disappear entirely, so she hangs on for dear life. "Don't leave me," "Please come back," and "Where were you?" are all cries for constant affirmation that this parent isn't going to leave her ever again.

Children who fear losing a parent often throw temper tantrums, keep up a steady steam of questions, cry, tell lies, or suddenly "don't feel good." They try anything they can to make sure Mommy or Daddy won't disappear. These children may also try to act like perfect children so their parent will give them more attention and they can remain attached. A child reasons that if she's the best little girl in the world, who wouldn't want to be with her constantly?

THE COPING MECHANISMS. Desiring to remain attached to someone is the coping mechanism for the fear of loss. It's not just the attachment this person craves, but the need to stay attached at all costs, and she will behave in any manner toward that goal. She carries over the fear of a parent going away and not returning. Trust doesn't come easily because she's afraid that no one she loves will return. She will want to be joined at the hip with her loved one as much as she can to keep the fear at bay. In some cases, this attachment can show up as extreme, and in other cases, it can be more subtle, but it's there.

In the opposite coping mechanism, the child simply won't engage, so there's no chance for loss to occur. If you don't want or need anything, there is nothing to lose—or so the theory goes. This child doesn't seem to care if her parent goes away or how often it happens, because she has buried her feelings deep inside and there is no way she is going to unveil them. Therefore, she has to act as if they don't exist in the first place. As an adult, she goes through life emotionally unattached to anyone or anything, but she pays a big price for her refusal to commit to placing a value on anything outside herself. This is similar to the coping mechanisms in the other fears in that detachment plays a huge part in many relationships and seems to be a large problem in relationships today as a result. In many relationships, one partner doesn't know their anniversary date or when the house payment is due or what the other's favorite color or dessert is. Social events are missed because a mate wasn't paying attention when the spouse announced the dates and times. Communication falls by the wayside because of detachment issues, and two people are left living together but not really knowing anything about each other.

CAN YOU SEE YOURSELF HERE? Look at these statements and see if you identify with any of them.

- You anticipate you will lose what's important to you in the end.
- You feel too dependent on others.
- You don't want to be dependent in any way.
- You don't feel you can count on anyone.
- You have problems saying no.

Don't pick yourself, or anyone else, apart if you see these fears being played out in your own or someone's else's life. We can all lay claim to fears; we wouldn't be human if we couldn't. Also, remember these fears took root in childhood when we were too young to understand what was going on and had only a limited amount of experience to deal with them. When something gets stuck in our minds when we're young, it wears a groove in our brains, and we keep repeating the same behaviors we did when we were children. Spotting our personal fears gives us a starting point from which we can work to lessen their impact on our lives.

What Does My Fear Look Like?

Complete the following exercise by giving a yes or no answer to each question. Think carefully about your answer and try to avoid making a snap decision. If your immediate answer comes from your gut, good, don't ignore it; but if it comes from your head because you don't want to be like that or to think you are like that, look a little deeper. Each question has two parts, the second part addressing fear.

1. Do you verbally or emotionally hurt your partner because he hasn't met your needs or you fear that he won't?
2. Do you need constant attention from him or fear that you do?
3. Do you hold on to your partner so tightly that he can't have a life of his own, or do you fear that you do?
4. Do you fear or think he's never there for you?
5. Do you feel detached from your partner or fear that you are?
6. Do you not want to talk about problems or fear that you don't?

7. Do you say "yes" when you mean "no," or vice versa, or fear that you do?
8. Do you pull him close and then push him away or fear that you do?
9. Do you fear saying "no" to a loved one or think you do?
10. Do you need lots of "alone time" away from your partner or fear that you do?
11. Do you think or fear that your partner is unreliable?
12. Do you emotionally distance yourself in relationships or fear that you do?
13. Do your actions toward your partner differ from what you really feel for him, or do you fear that they do?
14. Do you choose men who want to be with you all the time or fear that you do?
15. Do you need lots of togetherness or fear that you do?
16. Do you only think you are safe when you are with your partner or know what he is doing, or do you fear that you do?
17. Do you think or fear that you are too demanding of your partner?
18. Do you think or fear that you attend to your partner's needs but he doesn't reciprocate?
19. Do you devote your life and resources to him or fear that you do?
20. Do you fear or think that your partner is too emotional?
21. Do you push away from too much togetherness or fear that you do?
22. Do you always let your partner make the first move (in intimacy, after a fight, or in sharing feelings) or fear that you do?

23. Do you think or fear that your partner dislikes you?
24. Do you think of yourself as a clinger or fear that you are?
25. Do you think about or fear losing your partner?
26. Do you think or fear that you may be too independent in relationships?
27. Do you say "yes" more often than you say "no" or fear that you do?
28. Do you fear or think that you are overly dependent on your mate?
29. Do you do everything yourself because you can't count on your partner or fear that you can't?
30. Do you show physical affection to your partner more often than he does to you, or do you fear this is the case?
31. Do you pursue your partner and then back away or fear that you do?
32. Do you think or fear that your partner needs too much emotionally, physically, sexually, or financially?

Your answers to these questions help identify what coping mechanisms you are using in your life. Knowing where they came from and working through them gives you options in relating to your mate from an adult frame of mind without the childhood demons.

Finding Out What Type of Partner You Are

Now that you have started to identify your fears and coping mechanisms, you may begin to see how they mimic the connection you had with a parent and how they surface in your relationships now. If you answered "yes" three or more times in questions 1 through 8, you could be operating out of a fear of abandonment and should read the section titled "The Love Me/Don't Leave Me Partner." If you answered in the affirmative three or more times in questions 9 through 16, your fear may be about being smothered, so you should read "The Love Me/Don't Smother Me Partner." Answering "yes" three or more times in questions 17 through 24 points to rejection being your primary fear; you will want to read "The Love Me/Don't Discard Me Partner." Finally, if you agreed with three or more of questions 25 through 32, you exhibit a fear of loss; "The Love Me/Don't Go Away from Me Partner" is for you.

In the case of each of these fears, the underlying feeling—taken to an extreme—is that you are unworthy, unlikable, and unable to belong to anyone. Again, we all experience one or all of those feelings to some degree and on some level, but we don't have to accept it as our lot in life. What's interesting is that once we recognize what our fears are and how we deal with them, we can look at the type of person we draw into our lives and begin to predict his behavior as well. The payoff is then we can avoid men who can't or won't meet our needs, and we can move on to someone who is just right for us.

The Love Me/Don't Leave Me Partner

If your personal fear is that you will be abandoned and your defense against this fear, as a child, was to cling to the parent you were afraid would leave, you will attract someone who does not express his feelings and is emotionally and physically distant. Thus, you will feel abandoned all over again. This is like Susan, to whom I spoke on a radio show. She said, "My boyfriend won't tell me how he is feeling about our relationship and where he sees it going. I do everything I can to make him feel comfortable: I wash his clothes, cook him dinner, make all our social plans, and am available to him at all times. What else can I do?" The answer is not what else she can do for him. The feeling of having to cling to him to keep him from leaving speaks volumes about her fear of abandonment, and that is where the adjustment needs to be made. Sounds like that parent we just talked about, doesn't it?

If you chose the defense of detaching and not caring, you will hook up with someone who you feel is too severe and demanding and who wants all your time and attention, even if that is not the case in reality. You are so fearful of being left that you will not want to invest much in the relationship; therefore, you see your partner as wanting too much. If he wants you to block off every Sunday so the two of you can spend it together talking about your relationship—checking in, if you will—and having that time to be close with no outside distractions, you might see that as too much togetherness, on both an emotional and a physical level. It's understandable and desirable to want this part of a relationship, but you may think it borders on suffocation because you need lots of space. You might wonder (albeit subconsciously) why you would want to get close since you know the relationship is not going to last anyway. Here you've chosen someone who is the opposite of your parent. The opposite is the same really, just the other side of the coin.

With both of these responses, the feeling is "I know in the end it's not going to work and I'm going to be left." This is not a good message to bring into a relationship, but you don't have to live with this fear if you don't want to.

The Love Me/Don't Smother Me Partner

A fear of absorption or being smothered leads to either disengaging from loved ones or to outward acquiescence, which demands internally splitting off from feelings. You either push relationships away, or you surrender to them.

If you disengage, you will probably attract a partner who is physically and emotionally remote, because that person certainly isn't going to smother you. He will be too busy working or engaging in his hobbies or watching television or doing volunteer work to be available to interact with you. He has his own agenda and doesn't want you to crowd him in his pursuits. You can jump up and down or walk into the living room wearing your sexiest outfit, but if his favorite show is on—and he has many—he's not going to appreciate the interruption.

On the other hand, if you gave in to your parent and let him or her suffocate your individuality, you will have a tendency to succumb to any relationship that presents itself. If a man pursues you and is interested in a romantic relationship, you will give in because he's there. Not because you have looked to see who he is and what's he's really about, but just because he's there. Learning about him means you have to represent and stand up for yourself, and you don't do that. You didn't stand up and represent yourself with your parent because it wasn't allowed, and frankly, you don't even know how to do it. You give in to the inevitable; you are just going to be absorbed by him anyway. With this coping mechanism, you will be drawn to someone who may humiliate you or take total charge of the relationship just like your parent did long ago. For example, Becky's fiancé wants her to dress in suits all the time because that's what he likes, and she does this to please him. He wants to eat at the same restaurant every Friday night; she loves variety, but she goes along with his preference. He loves hiking which she dislikes, but she bought hiking boots and goes with him. As you can see, the fear of absorption can cause you to lose yourself to the other person in a relationship, and you may wonder at some point where you went. Seeing this fear played out in your life and changing tactics will save you lots of years of being invisible.

The Love Me/Don't Discard Me Partner

Fear of rejection is what stops many of us from doing what we really want to do in life. One of the greatest fears people have is public speaking because of the rejection factor. The feeling is that it's not safe to be visible because we open ourselves up for a negative response, and we don't want to take the chance of being dismissed as not good enough or likable enough.

On a personal level, it becomes, "What if I approach that good-looking man and he rejects me?" "What if I ask my honey to make love and he rejects me?" "What if I pour out my feelings and he tells me they're stupid?" These questions surface when you are operating out of the fear of rejection. You don't want to be exposed on a public or a personal level and run the risk of being found wanting in any way. Underneath the fear is the belief that you have an inherent flaw that will cause the rejection and that it is inevitable. If your coping mechanism is to avoid close emotional contact with others, you don't have to worry about being rejected because you'd never put yourself in any of the situations described here. You've rejected yourself, and you are now rejecting others by not trusting anyone to treat you with respect. Rejection is what you've come to expect, so you live it out in your relationships. You get involved with men who do reject you on some level or find you insufficient in some way. You are unable to read, in the beginning of a relationship, if the other person is capable of giving you validation. Without being able to read someone, you just get what you get. It's a shake of the dice, and often rejection is the name of the game.

On the other hand, if you cope by trying to be exactly what someone else wants, you might pick a partner you know you can take care of—someone who needs you and requires rescuing, whether from the small details of life or the bigger issues he is dealing with. If you can rescue him, your (subconscious) reasoning goes, he isn't going to reject you because you are helping him live his life in the best way possible. You're safeguarding your importance to him in the hope that rejection doesn't rear its ugly head.

Your main goal is obtaining approval and acceptance from others rather than getting it from yourself. When you do that, you hand others the power to accept or reject you based on who they are and their perceptions. This isn't really about you, it's about them. Natalie, one of my clients, said it clearly: "I was never the best-looking girl at school and wasn't accepted by the 'in' group, even though I got good grades and was a good student. I so needed my peers' acceptance—which I never got—that when I met a boy at a dance and he told me I was pretty *and* smart, I fell head over heels in love with him without looking at who he really was. We got married, and a year later we were divorced because he

found someone else. I'm devastated." Natalie found out that
looking for outside approval without having the skills to
determine if the other person can or wants to support you in
working through this need is a road riddled with pitfalls.

The Love Me/Don't Walk Away from Me Partner

The fear of loss appears as an attempt to remain attached
at all costs or to distance oneself emotionally to avoid the
feeling of loss. Having something valuable and losing it is
much worse than never having something of value in the first
place, or so the thinking of this fear goes.

Often people who are operating under this fear have an
unrealistic preoccupation with loss. If you've lost a child,
it's understandable that you would have that fear, but if you
haven't and worry unreasonably, it's an ungrounded fear and
rooted in the past. There's also a fine line between wanting
a valuable relationship to last and obsessively attempting to
hold on to it at all costs.

This fear manifests in several ways. You might make plans
for the distant future as a means of ensuring that loved ones
will still be around down the line. If you make arrangements
six months in advance, there is a false sense of security that
the relationship will still be intact then. It's like playing a
mind game with yourself. Another way fear of loss shows up
is in always being nice and of service to your partner. Janice
always offered to pick up her honey's clothes at the clean-
ers and entertain his business associates; she even offered to
take care of his children, mother, and Uncle Stu when the
occasions arose. This was her ploy to make herself so valuable to him, that he wouldn't leave her. The problem here is
that she has chosen someone who likes being the parent to

whom she plays the child who wants desperately to please. Alternatively, you might chose someone who is domineering and outspoken, who wants to be king of the castle, or who needs to be right all the time. This seems safe, but it doesn't give you an equal relationship in which you can be half of the equation with your own needs, wants, and desires.

Another manifestation of the fear of loss is to avoid engaging in any way. You might choose men who let you be so independent that there is really nothing much to your relationship except being roommates. My client Alison brought this to light when she said, "I have so much going on in my life that I hardly have any time for my husband. He doesn't seem to mind, but I'm beginning to. We seem to be nothing more than two people who contribute to the household expenses, and I'm starting to think I want more."

In this case, as Alison did, you pick a partner who has minimal relationship needs and is just as distant as you are. You have to be the one in charge because he is passive and wants others to be in control so he can detach. Since you believe you are never going to get your needs met, you put lots of emotional distance between you and feel safe—if lonely at times.

REBECCA:
PICKING ANOTHER
TYRANT LIKE DAD

Rebecca knew something was wrong with her, but she couldn't identify exactly what it was. First she thought it was her weight and the way her body looked. She didn't have a perfect body like her favorite actresses, and she used to beat herself up over that. She would start exercising and would feel better for a while, then the old feelings would return. She found other things to worry about—money, her career, making the right life choices, the way she treated her family—it was never-ending. She knew she had a flaw, but she just couldn't pinpoint it.

Rebecca moved from her parents' house to a dorm room at the university, then to a house that she and her fiancé found. She had never lived on her own and was afraid of doing so. On the outside she looked like she was independent, but underneath was the fear of rejection. At the beginning of their relationship, her fiancé seemed supportive, and she thought she was in love. Once they started living together, everything changed. He always seemed to know a better way of doing what she did and was constantly critical.

Her father had been the same type of person. He had always criticized her and tried to make her into the person he wanted her to be. He rejected most things about her and let her know in no uncertain terms what he expected. In her teenage years, he only let her wear certain clothes, she could only date certain boys, and her curfew was very strict or she'd suffer the consequences.

She was insightful enough to have the thought creep in every once in a while that perhaps she had become engaged to her dad. They might seem a bit different, as her fiancé didn't mind what she wore or who her friends were, but they both found things about her they didn't like and wanted to change. She is now working toward a better understanding of who she is and isn't and is beginning to confront her fiancé about his fault-finding nature. Rebecca is taking it slowly and doesn't know if he will join her on her path or if he needs to be in a relationship where he is the boss. Only time will tell.

***

All four of the fears we've discussed keep a relationship from being fully functional. If only one partner is doing the growing, the relationship is stuck where it is without a chance to improve. To move forward, both you and your partner need to see what kind of game each of you is playing and decide to change the rules. Then you can step out of the shadow of fear, turn the light on, and take the necessary steps to changing your relationship dynamics.

Dealing with Your Fears

To experience great relationships, you have to know how to deal with your own fears from the past so you don't keep repeating destructive behavior. Dealing with your fears offers you the opportunity to attract men into your life who understand and are perhaps also dealing (or have dealt) with their own fears and coping mechanisms. This is the best possible scenario for the two of you to work together in forming a strong bond that will deliver more happiness than you've ever had. Like attracts like, as you know. If you are in a relationship and do your own work, then the people around you have to change because you've changed your behavior and they must adjust to the new you.

Facing Abandonment Issues

If you've discovered that you have a fear of abandonment, it's important that you learn to trust wisely. Too many people give all their confidences right away at the beginning of a relationship, whether it's a friendly or a romantic one, then they get burned because they trusted too quickly. Don't trust blindly; let it develop. To build lasting faith in someone else, divulge a small piece of information about yourself and see what the other person does with it. If it's received the way you want it to be, then continue to open up slowly until you have a history of knowing how he or she is going to respond.

You can give trust, but you can also take it away if the other person does something unhealthy with it, such as throwing it back in your face or teasing you about personal information you've shared. Stop confiding when it doesn't feel good any longer. This gives you the power to invest (or not to invest) in this particular person. It's a simple process once you get the hang of it, and it will keep you from feeling unduly exposed to anyone.

You also have to work on knowing that good can come to you. Believe that the glass is half-full. Just because something negative happened in the past doesn't mean it's going to continue throughout your whole life. It's safe to believe that it will, because then you don't have to take risks, but without risks you'll never get a chance to see how great life can be when you aren't holding on to your safety blanket. I love affirmations and looking at what I have to be grateful for each day. You can always find something that you enjoyed or that was a good experience. Maybe the person at Starbucks gave you a bright smile or you found the perfect parking place. Keep building on those positive experiences until you believe good things are there for you each and every day.

Facing Absorption Issues

If you fall into the fear-of-being-absorbed category, there are certain steps you can take to come out from under this cloud. You will want to work toward an interdependent relationship. In this type of relationship, both partners are vulnerable and dependent on each other in a positive way. It's not about one person being exposed and the other taking advantage, but about two people working together for the common good of the relationship. The needs will shift back and forth with both people giving and taking during the course of the relationship. There is a flow to this dynamic rather than having two people stuck in prescribed roles.

You also have to learn to get in touch with feelings that may have been pushed aside or buried a long time ago. To this end, it's a good idea to write down your feelings about situations that arise in your everyday life. How did it feel when a coworker snubbed you, or what was your emotional reaction when your child said, "I love you"? Did heavy traffic cause you to be anxious or angry? What was your positive or negative reaction to your mother's comments about your outfit? You might not be able to name a specific feeling in every situation, but the more you practice, the easier it will get. Don't pass judgment on whatever feelings you have. You can decide what to do with them later, but for now, just knowing what they are is a step in the right direction.

Once you are comfortable with your feelings, you are less apt to go along with what a partner wants or says just for the sake of pleasing him. You will want to keep the real you in the relationship as much as you can, and this is good. Once you learn to hold on to that personal part of you, you'll never go back to doing it the old way again.

Facing Rejection Issues

The fear of rejection hits most of us to some degree and can hamper our progress through life. To combat this fear, look closely at the erroneous message you picked up early on that says you have a flaw. We all have our strengths and weaknesses, but those weaknesses, whatever they are, don't represent a flaw. You don't want to believe you have a defect and project that belief to others; if you act as if they know about some flaw in you and will judge you harshly, it becomes a self-fulfilling prophecy.

For example, you may think your partner is too emotional and assume that he thinks you are not emotional enough. You know that your parents were emotionally repressed, so any expression of his feelings seems like a volcanic eruption. When any of your own feelings surface, you may make fun of them or apologize for them. In time, you will convince your partner that you are not emotional, which is not the total truth, but you think showing emotions is a defect you have. You then believe he has the opposite defect of being too emotional. To break this cycle, look at what you think your flaw is and really examine it. Is it really a major defect or just a garden-variety weakness? You may choose to work on this perceived flaw or simply accept it and move on from there.

If you are uncomfortable with lots of togetherness and your partner wants more, start working slowly toward more couple time. Add another hour here or another day there. Take baby steps so you can reach a compromise with your mate. It doesn't have to be totally his way, but it doesn't have to be totally your way either. Meeting in the middle is what healthy relationships are all about.

To face the fear of rejection, you also need to know that it's OK to have needs. In a healthy relationship, each of you has your own needs, not to the exclusion of the other person's but in a way that allows you to work together. Maybe your need is to go skiing every weekend in the winter and your partner doesn't want to do this. It's OK to go by yourself and let him stay home and enjoy the weekend on his own, or maybe you can reach a compromise and go twice a month for the season. Neither is right or wrong as long as each partner's needs are honored. This arrangement gives you a separate sense of yourself, which is imperative to having a happy, strong relationship.

Facing Loss Issues

If you have a fear of loss, you may attach yourself fiercely to your partner just as you did with your parent in the hope that he won't disappear entirely. The lesson you may need to learn is where you end and your mate begins. You don't want to be in a symbiotic relationship in which you either depend on someone too much or are deathly afraid of being too needy. When you learn your boundaries—which you may have to do with the help of a therapist depending on the severity of your fear—you are able to represent yourself in a relationship and not get lost in it. You know when you can count on yourself, and you know when you can count on your partner. Once you realize that dependence doesn't have to mean a loss of your identity or a loss of a partner, the fear will stop rearing its ugly head.

Instead of giving in to the anticipation of losing what's really important to you, you can turn that around and believe you can have what you want in life and it won't be taken away. Think of what you have wanted in life and have actually gotten, whether it's a high school or college diploma, a great job, children you love, an interest you adore, or a body you have worked to get the way you like it. Any big or small achievement should be on this list to prove to yourself that yes, you can have something and not lose it. Of course, unforeseen circumstances may have caused a loss that was beyond your control. Don't count that as something you lost; we're talking about what you do have control over. If you picked the wrong man and lost that relationship, it was your selection process that got in the way and not some predetermined programming that said you have to lose what you want. This process is completely under your control. You can start learning what to look for the next time around and make a better choice.

Another idea to understand is that all relationships have an ebb and flow. Some may be around all your life—maybe you still have friends from preschool—but many of those friends have gone their separate ways, and you have also. This is normal and, to most of us, simply a way of life. You might have had a best friend in high school or college you rarely see any longer. Some people come into our life stories for just a few chapters, and that's OK. Perhaps they were there to teach us a lesson of some sort or to help us through a rough time. Often it's difficult for a friendship to endure all the changes two people go through over the years, and there's nothing wrong with that. Don't count a discontinued relationship as a loss that proves you can't have anything you want. Look at it as a learning experience, face forward, and move on to the next chapter in your life.

To whatever degree you experience a fear in your life, you have the opportunity to do something to change that fear. You need to identify it, face it directly, and then decide that it isn't going to affect your life any longer. Maybe Mom and Dad helped it along when you were young, but you don't have to stay under its influence and power. You are going to learn to disregard it and put something positive in its place, moving away from parent-based relationships. Remember that car that was a lemon and wouldn't get you where you wanted to go so you traded it in on a new model that was better suited to your needs? That's what you are going to do with your fears. Trade them in for what you do want out of life. Now that you have this knowledge under your belt and know what to do with your fears, it's important to be able to identify the type of relationship you want and how that matches up to what you have.

4

You Say You Want Vanilla and You Chose Spumoni

Finding Out What You Want and Seeing Clearly What You Really Have

We identified what type of partner you are attracted to in Chapter 2, and in Chapter 3, we discussed the fears you operate under and how both your partners and fears are part of the parent trap. This information is helping you be a more savvy shopper, but exactly what type of relationship are you shopping for? Relationships are front and center for all of us. You can be in any of the following situations:

- *In a relationship* of some kind whether it's permanent and has staying power or is short term
- *Moving toward a relationship*, thinking about one, or planning one
- *Moving away from relationships*, wanting to distance yourself because they have been painful, disappointing, and/or unsatisfying in the past
- *Putting relationships on hold* because they don't fit into your life at the moment (In this case, you haven't given up on them, but you aren't moving toward one either.)

Whether we love them, avoid them, or yawn when we think about them, relationships make the world go around. In this chapter, you'll figure out what your relationship style is and if that style is really right for you. Are the relationships you've had the ones you always dreamed of? Or did you get waylaid somewhere along the way by playing out your "relationship script" based on past conditioning? You will have the chance to ask yourself if you are headlining a new production all your own or merely playing an extra in the same old family drama. If you find yourself in the third category and are moving away from relationships, the information you are learning in this book will answer questions as to why your relationships in the past have been less than positive and why you have put distance in that area of life. Heck, you might even want to venture out there and try again, but with different results this time; and then again, you might just want the information and understanding as to why you took this path. If you have put relationships on hold, this new information will be very beneficial when you decide to open that door once again. You will be better equipped to sort through the men that show up, resulting in an even better relationship than you have had in the past. It's amazing how understanding changes the results so dramatically if you decide to put into practice what you've learned. Relationship limits can be erased and you can soar with the best of them in this area.

What's Your Relationship Style?

In today's society, you can have almost any type of relationship you want, whether it's living together without legal paperwork, living just down the block from each other, or being wed and living on opposite sides of the country. No longer do you have to be the "little lady" and play out the traditional role of a dutiful housewife. If that works for you, great, but there are ways to have a great relationship other than what our grandparents knew. Having this freedom in relationships means society has changed for the better, giving everyone more options than ever before.

This section describes different love matches and asks you to determine which one you gravitate toward. There is always a main theme in a relationship, and while you may fit one category perfectly, you may have a more complex relationship that combines two or more. For example, Sally, a call-in on a radio show, asked me why she kept thinking and fantasizing about men other than her husband. She said she and her husband got along fine and talked about everything that happened to them each day, but something was missing for her. Friends envied them their marriage, and she thought she was crazy to be feeling the way she did. After more conversation, it came out that on the surface their marriage looked great, but they had no emotional connection and that was showing up in the bedroom. They had sex, but she didn't get much out of it; in fact, she was bored. Sally and her husband had settled into a maintenance relationship, and she was discovering that it really didn't work for her. Whether it's high maintenance (which some can be), competitive, or just plain elusive, your relationship follows a pattern. In Chapter 6, we'll look at the details for a healthy relationship, but now let's look at the various types.

Depending on the people involved, each of the seven styles of relationships will either work fine or restrict, damage, and limit one or both partners. A certain type of relationship may be best for one couple based on how they function emotionally, whereas for others, the same type of relationship would be like a death sentence for who they really are and want to be.

It's all about knowing what works for you on a gut level and not just living out your fantasies about what you think should work. There's a big difference between the two, and you need to learn what these differences are. Getting to your real heart's desires and not being caught in the parent trap is what allows you to have an ongoing love with another person. As you read through this section, try to determine where you fit in.

- *A maintenance relationship.* Both partners are comfortable living parallel lives and are not interested in any growth or emotional closeness.
- *A parent/child relationship.* One partner has the authority in the relationship, and the other tries to please him or her.
- *A competitive relationship.* Each partner tries to one-up the other.
- *A rescuing relationship.* One partner is in need of saving—whether physically or emotionally—and the other gladly takes on the role of caretaker.
- *A distant relationship.* The two partners live apart because they don't want to deal with the day-to-day issues in a relationship.
- *A possessive relationship.* One partner clings to the other, and the other feels safe in that possessiveness.
- *A working relationship.* Both partners work together for the common good of the relationship, and it continues to evolve and grow over time.

There is a mutual dependency in each of these relationships as each person depends on the other to maintain his or her position. Problems arise when one person moves on from the prescribed role and the other doesn't, or when the dynamic of the relationship prevents one or both partners from growing. My client Jennifer was thinking about breaking up with her longtime boyfriend and wasn't sure she was doing the right thing. He had many great qualities but refused to discuss making the relationship permanent with a marriage license. He kept saying that he didn't want to spoil what they had by moving in together and that he needed his space more than he thought marriage would allow.

Jennifer wanted to start a family and was beginning to see that it wasn't going to happen with him. She was perplexed at this continued response from him and had started pushing even more for a wedding ring. Now he wasn't coming over as much as he had in the past, and she didn't know what to do. Should she leave him alone and go back to the way things were, keep pushing, or break it off? Without knowing it, Jennifer had changed the dynamics in their relationship and was no longer the "go-with-the-flow" girl her boyfriend used to know. She was ready to move on, and he wasn't. She did end the relationship and is looking for a great man who will give her what she wants.

As long as two people continue on the path that was set up at the beginning, the relationship can hum along nicely, but if one strays from that path, trouble is brewing. To assist you in determining which type of relationship you have traditionally chosen and subconsciously agreed to, take a look at the more detailed descriptions of each style.

Maintenance Relationships

This type of relationship works well for two people who don't want to bond emotionally or exclusively. They go with the flow and don't have much need for a more intimate connection. They might be afraid of closeness and the rejection that this could bring—not wanting to upset what they have because it's better than anything they've had in the past—or they might want to avoid putting in the time and effort to move the relationship to a different level.

A maintenance relationship can be comfortable if both partners stay where they are and have their needs met. The problem arises if one wants more and is not willing to address this with the other. Often this type of relationship looks perfect to outsiders, but in reality, it's not that great. The distance in this relationship type allows for secrets such as gambling, substance abuse, or affairs while still maintaining the status quo between the partners—at least for the time being.

Brad and Martha: Together and Apart at the Same Time

All their friends admired the relationship Brad and Martha had. They lived in an upscale neighborhood, had the clothes and cars to match, took wonderful vacations, and enjoyed attending cultural events together. What their friends didn't see was that the only things they ever talked about were the house, what trip they were going on next, how they liked the last opera they saw, or whose party they were going to the following weekend. There was never any talk of feelings, fears, or concerns, and sex was simply a physical routine for them when they got around to it, which wasn't often. If their friends could have seen that there wasn't much in the way of emotional intimacy between Brad

and Martha, they might not have admired the relationship so much, but it worked for Brad and Martha and
they were content with it the way it was.

Parent/Child Relationships

This style of relationship is set up so that one partner has all
the authority over and responsibility for the other. For the
one who takes the parent role, it's like having a child, and he
or she infantilizes the other person. This is unlike the rescuing relationship, in which each partner sees the other as an
adult. The parent/child relationship locks people into the two
roles because the "parent" won't let the "child" become more
independent. We have all seen or at least heard of the mom
who has a hard time letting go of her child and tries everything she can to keep the child dependent on her. In either
case, this dynamic works for both people involved as long
as they both want it to. The problem comes in if either the
parent grows tired of the responsibility or the child decides
he or she wants more independence and tries to break free of
the constraints that have been imposed.

DENNIS AND MARY:
STAYING IN
THEIR ROLES

During their twenty-year marriage Mary had
never earned how to drive. Dennis was always
going to teach her but never seemed to get around
to it. After a while, it became a nonissue, and Mary

depended on Dennis to take her to the grocery store, doctor's appointments, and most other places. He would drop her off at the mall and then pick her up at a specified time and place. She had never worked outside the home, and Dennis liked it that way. He always knew where she was and what she was doing. It was like a parent and a child, and they both accepted the roles they had assumed.

Mary sewed for others, so she was able to socialize with her customers and even went to bingo once a week with a friend who was a former customer. Another friend gave her a ride to church on Sundays. She was happy with her life and her marriage; she liked having someone else make the decisions in the family so she could live without any undue stress. Both Dennis and Mary were content with the relationship they had.

Competitive Relationships

A competitive relationship occurs when the two people involved enjoy scoring off of each other. It's like the song that goes, "Anything you can do, I can do better. I can do anything better than you." This can take the form of a friendly competition in which one partner says to the other, "Hey, you did well on that one. Now I'm going to try to better that." In a functional competitive relationship, each person wishes the other success in all endeavors. The couple is supportive and loving, and they make competition a fun game.

At the other extreme lies the couple who compete to make themselves feel better, each always wanting to feel superior to the other and to show him or her up. It becomes a game of one-upmanship where no one really wins. One partner always has to be inferior so that the other can feel more competent. It's just like that friend who always has to have a better car or house or relationship than you do. In some couples there is a person who always loses and in other relationships each partner "loses" sometimes.

JONATHAN AND JANICE: WANTING TO BE THE BEST

Jonathan and Janice met at a golf course. They were assigned to the same foursome and found that they enjoyed trying to outdo each other. They started making bets between them on who would get the better score on each hole. They agreed that the winner at the end was to treat the loser to dinner at a nice place. When Janice won, Jonathan graciously allowed her choose the restaurant that they would go to the following week. She made her selection, and they set the date.

During dinner, Janice's cell phone kept ringing, and some of the calls she felt she had to take because they were business related. She also wanted to show Jonathan how important she was and that maybe she was even more important than he was. He wouldn't be outdone and started talking about taking the company jet to Europe the following day for some business dealings of his own. They dated for several months, but one was always trying to impress the other, and they couldn't seem to get past that. Each of them wanted to be seen as more valuable than the other, whether it was in business, sports, or knowing all the words to certain songs. The relationship was set up as a competition in all areas, and neither partner could let go of that dynamic.

Rescuing Relationships

This type of relationship meets the needs of two people who want to play out the roles of needy partner and savior. One person has something to be fixed, such as an addiction, an emotional problem, a financial crisis, or a physical impairment, and the other steps in as rescuer and caretaker. The rescuer sees the other partner as an adult, albeit an inadequate or inept one. This type of relationship is commonly referred to as codependent.

If the rescuing is mutual, this can be a functional relationship. For example, one partner may have financial problems and the other is comfortable supplying most of the needed income; however, the financially unstable partner does everything to repair and maintain the house because the other partner doesn't know how. Each of them is codependent on the other, but it works for their relationship. One person can start earning more money or the other one can learn to fix the faucet, and it won't change their relationship.

In other cases, both partners need to stay in their assigned roles so that neither ever has to change. The fixer is dependent on the fixee to maintain his or her problem so the fixer can always be there either to put things right or to cover it up and stay in the position of control. The fixee is dependent on the fixer to allow him or her to maintain the imperfection and not have to deal with and eradicate it alone.

For example, a man who can't keep a job has a wife who might complain about his earning power as she works and supports the family. He doesn't have to work, and she can feel superior. If he went out and found a great-paying job, this relationship could fall apart in no time.

Barry and Catherine: Guaranteeing Nothing Changed

Barry knew he was overweight, and his doctors even classified him as obese. He didn't know why Catherine had been attracted to him or why she had agreed to marry him, but she had. He hoped she would stay around and not leave him for someone who was in better shape. What he wasn't seeing was that Catherine kept baking pastries and leaving them in plain sight; she brought home leftovers from the potlucks at work and filled the refrigerator with them. She loved a well-stocked pantry, and there wasn't a bare spot in it.

Catherine had little self-confidence and needed Barry to stay the way he was so he wouldn't notice how inadequate she was and leave her for someone else. As long as he stayed grossly overweight and she accepted that, she felt safe in the relationship. They were both afraid of the other leaving or changing the dynamics between them, so the codependent relationship that centered on food and weight continued.

Distant Relationships

A distant relationship comprises two people who like the idea of being in a relationship but don't need or want the day-today complications of it. Each lives in another city, state, or country and only seeing each other occasionally works out fine. They may talk every day and share the details of their lives, but they don't have to worry about taking turns with the housework or what they are going to do with a free Sunday. If a bad mood strikes one of them, they simply end the phone call early and don't have to confront how they take their mood out on the other.

Every time they get together it's vacation time, and all is well with the world. It's like having the honeymoon part of a relationship over and over. This couple doesn't need to sort out their differences and personal relationship issues. They each get to have their own personal life and experiences, and basically do as they wish. If it works for both of them and they don't want to change, they could stay like this for the long haul.

Some people, though, have a distant relationship and then decide to live together. That's usually when the trouble starts, because they haven't dealt with the details. Seeing each other every weekend or once a month is quite different than living with someone every day, week after week.

FRANK AND TERRI: LIVING THE HONEYMOON LIFE

Living on opposite sides of the country seemed to work for Frank and Terri. They would take turns flying out to see each other once a month and talk on the phone and exchange e-mails on a consistent basis. When vacation time rolled around, they would pick a spot they both loved and meet there. For the most part, these meetings were filled with laughter and great sex. Of course, they both experienced life's ups and downs, but they tried to keep the negative moods to a minimum because it was such a treat to spend time together in person.

They talked about one moving to live with the other, but they knew that would require more adjustments than they were willing to make. Terri had become a vegetarian and stayed up late, working and reading. She was a night person. Frank was the opposite and needed his early bedtime and total silence. She liked to attend parties and openings, and he relished staying home with his cat, to which she was allergic. They couldn't make it together, but apart they were great friends, and that's really all they both wanted—to have someone to say, "Hi" to and talk about what went on that day, then to have the rest of their time to do as they pleased.

Possessive Relationships

This relationship style involves one partner who clings to the other for a sense of security, while the other partner derives a feeling of satisfaction from being the protector. The clinging partner is often insecure; this may be apparent or this person may have a great professional life and look secure to the world but be completely different at home. This person doesn't know what he or she wants unless the stronger partner says what it is.

Clingers need a protector to give form to who they are because they have so many self-doubts; they look to their partner for identity and value and only feel secure when their protector is directing and giving guidance. Protectors have a sense of self-importance based on the power they hold over a partner who can be molded. With all the emphasis on the clinger, the protector doesn't have to look at any of his or her own issues.

VICTOR AND ALICE: MAKING EACH OTHER FEEL IMPORTANT

Victor is Alice's possession, make no mistake about that. If any female comes within a short radius of Victor, and Alice is around, she's going to be right there protecting her property. Victor, knowing how he is supposed to act, will gladly welcome Alice into the conversation and will put his arm around her or hold her hand to let the other woman know that Alice is the only one in his life. Of course, the woman who walked up to him didn't have a thought of enticing him away from his wife or even flirting with him; she was just being friendly.

Neither Victor nor Alice wants anyone interfering or even thinking about coming between them. Alice helps Victor by giving him a sense of belonging as he doesn't have much self-esteem or confidence and depends on her to give him a sense of self-worth. Victor allows Alice to be the one in control of the relationship, which makes her feel safe because she doesn't have to think about changing anything about herself. Victor loves her just the way she is because she takes care of him.

Working Relationships

A working relationship is the ideal, although not everyone is ready for it. In this type of partnership, there are no set roles, and the couple is able to evolve. It's what we all strive for—in our thoughts, if not in our behavior. These two people recognize their childhood wounds and have made a commitment to work together to face these issues and get as far away from them as possible. There are still arguments and disagreements, but they are of the healthy variety, and understanding and resolution result. Both partners are willing to look at their weaknesses and shortcomings, to acknowledge when they may have fallen back into childhood behavior in their dealings with the other, and to address the problem and move forward. There is a give-and-take while they sort out what each is contributing to the relationship. Over time, the partners can become what they both secretly wanted in the first place—loving, supportive, kind partners who value and trust each other.

MARK AND BETTY: IN A RELATIONSHIP FOR ALL THE RIGHT REASONS

This was Mark's second marriage and Betty's third, and they were determined to make it a happy one. They had made a pact with each other that they would be honest; share their feelings, struggles, and doubts; and be kind, supportive, and loving through it all. They were committed to growth and were willing to do what it took to achieve that goal.

Of course, they had disagreements and they didn't always like each other, but they were both willing to work through any issues that came up. They recognized it was a lot of work, but they also saw the happiness that could be achieved in the intimacy they were striving for. They were a team, and it felt good. Betty is learning to consult with Mark before making any major decisions, which is something she didn't do with either of her previous husbands. Mark is learning to control his anger and talk things out rather than getting mad and leaving. It's a different kind of relationship than either has ever known, and they are thankful that it came into their lives when they were ready for it.

Keeping Both Eyes Open

The degree to which each partner plays his or her role is also a factor in the functionality of each type of relationship. For example, you may have an element of the parent/child relationship in that he fills your car up with gas every week for you and does all the grocery shopping. In a more extreme case, he may tell you what to wear, what to cook, when to go to bed, and what activities you should be involved in. When you are looking at these relationship types, keep this in mind: don't necessarily rule one out because it's not blatantly obvious.

You also need to look at the cost to you outside of the relationship. The relationship role you are playing out may work in your romantic relationship, but it may cost you as an individual by not allowing you to grow beyond that role in your interaction with others. If you are being taken care of in your relationship, you are probably looking for friends or coworkers who will take care of you as well. It becomes a way of life for you, and others may resent having to deal with your neediness. If you are the caretaker, you may try to fulfill that role with other people only to find that they don't want or need to be taken care of, and it could backfire on you when they confront you about it.

People don't start out in destructive relationships—far from it. No one would say, "Gee, I'm going to fall for this guy who is going to compete with me every step of the way to show me how superior he is, and it's going to be uncomfortable, and I'm going to hate it." Instead, you fall for the person you think (subconsciously, of course) can help you heal your past. He is going to be just like Mom or Dad in not giving you what you need. He is going to bring up all your issues, so that you can look at them and then decide whether you want to heal them with him. You can try, if you think you can succeed, or you can move on and do it with someone else. It's all up to you.

What Are Your Relationship Expectations?

In thinking about or planning stages of a relationship, it's important to know what the expectations and boundaries are going to be for a certain type of relationship and to ascertain if that works for you or not. Be very clear and up-front with yourself on this because your future comfort and happiness level with a partner will be determined by you knowing what works for you in the long run and what doesn't. This one step will make mate selection so much easier and more rewarding.

If you are currently in a relationship, knowing what the boundaries and expectations are will answer your questions as to why you and your partner have the dynamics you do. You will also know if they are set in stone or if they are more malleable. You will be able to answer the question, "Is it me or is it him or is it us together?" Sometimes once you know what guidelines you are playing with you can accept the way they are and live with them. If you can't live with them you can address the dynamics and see if changes can be made.

Once you have figured out how you like your relationships, you can learn what boundaries have been established and what the unspoken expectations are. For instance, if you prefer a maintenance relationship, it is probably pretty clear that there isn't going to be any great emotional involvement between the two of you. You've chosen to keep the status quo and not rock the boat, to maintain a rather quiet existence. To facilitate this, you have to choose someone who doesn't have a lot of enthusiasm for life and is afraid to take big risks. This isn't to say that this type of relationship doesn't work for a number of people who like to play it safe, but it wouldn't be the first choice for others.

The parent/child relationship requires both partners to stay within the boundaries of their particular roles and never vary. The "parent" may have always had to take care of someone—perhaps a parent or siblings—so he or she is comfortable doing this. The "child" has always been treated like a child and knows nothing else. This person may have become emotionally arrested while growing up and is still operating at that same age, whether it's three or twelve. To make this relationship work, you have to choose someone who always operates on an uneven playing field and doesn't know there's another way of relating.

In a competitive relationship, there is little support for either partner. It's all about one person winning and the other losing. It's always a win/lose situation; win/win is not a possibility. What you need to make this relationship tick is someone who plays the same "I'm better than you" game, someone who might acknowledge something positive about you and in the next breath take it away so he remains the victor. This occurs whether one partner consistently loses or if both partners lose occasionally. Someone is always the victor.

In a rescuing relationship, one person feels good because he or she is saving the other; the rescuee feels bad because he or she needs to be saved. Of course, that doesn't mean the flawed partner wants to change—there's no need, because the rescuer is there to take care of everything. Sometimes the rescuee really does change, but that throws off the dynamics and disrupts the flow of the relationship. Because this could easily end the relationship, one of you has to have a problem and one of you has to feel good about handling it.

In a distant relationship, both partners are emotionally detached. There are many pretend marriages out there that look like the real thing—at least they have papers to prove it—but they are empty relationships as far as any real connecting goes. In this case, you need, want, and must have your own space to keep from getting swallowed up in a relationship.

A possessive relationship needs a possessor and a possessee. The possessor could be the jealous type, controlling, selfish, domineering, and/or overprotective. He or she must find someone who accepts this type of behavior and even interpret it as caring, depending on the possessee's background. In a working relationship both people have to be willing to grow and change and adapt to each other. Sometimes this is easy to do and at other times it's uncomfortable to work through the issues that arise, but each are willing to do the work it takes. The two people have to be secure enough to be able to set their own needs aside at times for the good of the relationship.

Often in each relationship type, the position or role each person fulfills is set in stone and cannot be changed if the relationship is to remain intact. The position of each person and the style of the relationship is set at the beginning, so be aware that you're not going to "change him" down the road. This is one of the most common misconceptions—that changing a person is possible. What you see at the start is what you'll usually get stuck with. There is no going back, so buyer beware!

In a few cases, your partner might be willing to go into therapy and make some major changes in himself; that's great for both of you if you are also willing to make the changes you need to grow with him. Some relationships have more breathing space and can be renegotiated to benefit both partners without the change being seen as a threat. If that's your situation, congratulations, you've picked a winner!

What Style Does You Justice?

Daydream for a minute about the perfect relationship for you. What does it look and feel like? Is that the one you have or are looking for? Is your present relationship or the one you seem to keep attracting doing justice to your dream? A problem arises when you say you want one type of relationship but attract or are attracted to another type.

Margo told me that she'd always wanted someone who would make her laugh; her childhood had been somber and she didn't want to repeat that. Her idea of a perfect relationship revolved around lightness and amusement. The men she was attracted to made her laugh but were also little boys at heart whom she ended up mothering. Sure they were funny, but she was finding men who needed a somber mom to keep them in check so they could be productive members of society. Margo wasn't finding the lightness and amusement that she wanted after all.

Look at your own relationship desires. Do you dream about a relationship where the two of you are intellectual equals and have fascinating conversations? Maybe your daydream is of the two of you traveling around the world, having wonderful experiences wherever you go. Or you might dream about each of you contributing half to eventually buying a home and saving enough for an early retirement. Your dream man could be the one who talks about how he feels and listens to you when you do the same. Or you might support and encourage each other to pursue your interests. The daydream is all yours, and you get to decide all the details of it. Are you ready for that dream relationship?

Now keep your dream in mind as you read over the following questions. They are examples of how we often fantasize about one type of relationship but live in one that is quite different.

- Do you say you want intimacy in a relationship but don't really know what that entails and choose partners who don't know either?

- Do you want to make your own decisions in relationships but find yourself attracted to partners who handle the purse strings and prevent you from being an adult?
- Do you love aggressive men but fight with them all the time, leaving no opportunities for the two of you to grow together as a couple?
- Do you choose partners you have to mother and then get irritated at them because your idea of a partnership is one of equality?
- Do you attract men who can't make a full commitment even though you thought that's what you wanted?
- Are you attracting partners who want to be joined at the hip when you believe you value your independence?
- Do you draw in passive partners and then get angry when they won't stand up for themselves because you wanted a working relationship?
- Do authoritative partners come into your life and turn you into a second-class citizen when you dream of a nice, calm, give-and-take relationship?
- Do you think you are looking for an equal partnership and yet go for partners who need to be in control?
- Do you fall for men who want you to be in control, which you love and resent at the same time because it doesn't allow you to experience the balanced relationship you thought you wanted?
- Do your partners need a lot of space even though you say you want closeness?
- Do you find yourself involved with partners who don't or can't talk about feelings whereas you feel you can?
- Do all the men you meet seem to have some kind of fault that you have to fix when you really thought you wanted to spend time pursuing your own interests?

- Do men want to protect and take care of you, boring you because you want to be seen as an adult woman who is able to handle her own life?
- Has sex become dull, and does something hold you back from talking about it with your partner?
- Do you find men around whom you have to be on your guard and always on top of things, whether it's keeping the house clean, entertaining well, making sure the children are well behaved, or looking your best at all times when you thought you wanted a partner with whom you could stroll through the forest hand in hand, talking about your deepest thoughts and wishes?

Sometimes you can have specific relationship expectations and end up with something completely different. Other times relationships that appear to be everything you always wanted on the surface really prevent you from living the life you dreamed. Often the same roles that keep you content in a relationship also hinder you from moving forward and can even lead to vicious cycles with your partner. For example, in a rescuing relationship you might be OK, most of the time, with having a partner who has a problem. Then there may be times when either he crosses some line you have determined is there or something is happening in your own life that makes you less tolerant. When life gets back to normal you are OK once again only to have something else crop up and you are back to your relationship not being OK. You go around and around in this circle but never seem to get out of it.

Thinking about and answering these questions can show you why and how you are not getting your inner needs met. With this information, you can get a clearer picture of your

relationship agenda and see where you may be choosing partners unwisely. It's all about educating yourself in the ways of
relationships, both personally and generally.

Competitiveness shows up in *all* relationships to some
degree. One person needs to stay in a certain role and tries
to mandate that the other person stay in his or hers, but most
of the time it's not that easy. What usually results is that they
start acting like they are in a contest as to who plays their
role best or makes the other stay in their role. For example,
a refusal to be intimate pits the partner who wants the intimacy against the one who is resisting it, and back and forth
they go. Each one wants to win the challenge and have the
relationship their way. Or a couple who is all about power
may have one partner who allows the other to have conrol
and then tries to take it back. A competition is set up with
a winner and loser which is a far cry from a healthy working relationship. In a healthy, working relationship competitiveness is seen as a healthy aspect and is treated more as a
fun game, with neither partner the better person because of
the win.

Ron and Alice:
Meeting Their Own
Needs but Not
Each Other's

Ron is very supportive of his wife, Alice. He takes
her arm when crossing the street, and he worries
about her when she gets in the car to drive to the grocery store. In fact, he doesn't want her to have even one

worrisome thought and will tell her she's wrong about something that's making her depressed so *she* feels better—all within the guise of caring so much about her.

Alice came from a home in which she had to grow up too early, supporting her mother both physically and emotionally by taking care of her younger siblings. Alice's childhood need to be taken care of manifests in her current relationship. On the surface, she is getting the support from Ron she didn't get from her mother, but looking closer, it's not really support based on her needs, but rather a way for Ron to control the situation and make it comfortable for him. On one hand, Alice enjoys the mothering, but on the other, she doesn't like the feeling that she isn't competent to take care of herself. She goes along with it to a certain extent but is in competition with Ron about it at the same time. He wants her to call him when she gets to a friend's house, and she takes her power back by "forgetting" to do it. It's become a game of who's going to win each round.

Ron is acting out his father's role in the family and has married his mother, who was also a needy little girl. Alice's needs really don't come into play; it's his need to control, just like his dad did, which is producing the dynamic at work in their relationship. Alice doesn't realize she's married her mom, and Ron doesn't realize he has as well. It feels good for both of them as long as they don't delve any deeper into it—for now, at least. Down the road may be a different story.

It is important to see what type of relationship you have and then be able to identify what type you want. Perhaps you're ready to take the plunge and work toward the working relationship. Perhaps you recognize your role in a maintenance relationship and realize that you are happy for now. Again, it's all about choices, whether it's a new pair of shoes or a mate who fits your needs. We are bombarded with choices all over the place: Should we have granola or scrambled eggs for breakfast, a white car or a blue one, no children or six? If you know what you want relationshipwise, what works for you above and beyond all the fears and insecurities, and how to choose a partner who meets your needs, your relationship can truly be one of the best parts of your life. You go, girl!

You can become skilled at seeing whether you are sabotaging your choices and what you need to fulfill the quest for your dream relationship—as long as those dreams are based on reality, that is. Not that personal reality comes easy to a lot of us, but that is going to be changed by learning about leaving the past in the past and becoming savvy in emotional banking.

5

Get Rid of the Parental Skeleton in Your Closet

Moving Away from
Parent-Based Relationships

Having a relationship that reflects who you are and does not simply repeat the way your parents did relationships is what love is all about. Toward that end, you have to eliminate the old messages and shift to new messages that are going to meet your personal needs. This chapter assists you to that place in life by identifying emotional problems left over from childhood and enlightenment in judging the emotional investment made by both partners.

This chapter looks at rating a partner's qualities, checking out not only his availability, but also your own to determine the compatibility between the two of you. You will learn if both of you are sabotaging the relationship and determine if change is something that can occur. It's important to know the positive qualities for any given relationship, but you also have to be aware of the limitations that are there as all relationships have those also. Cinderella might just have been surprised when her Prince Charming left his shoes right in front of the door where she kept tripping over them.

Different qualities are needed for different types of relationships; so when you have determined what type of connection you want with another person you then need to know what qualities to look for in a mate and which ones should make you say, "This one is not for me." You need information to assess if the person next to you can even come close to providing what you need, or if you have a decision to make regarding your married or single status.

Emotional Economics

In exactly the same way you decide how much you can afford in mortgage payments for a new house, you have to decide how much you have to emotionally invest in a relationship and how that copies your past with your parents. Then you have to ascertain how much your partner has to invest and whether this level matches your needs. Your parents may have looked like they were emotionally committed, but truth be known, it was a veneer without much substance underneath. Your subconscious believes the picture they showed you is the way a relationship is supposed to be.

If they were kind and loving one day, and the next day they were frazzled from work and wanted you out of their sight, you might fool yourself into thinking they were emotionally there for you—at least, most of the time—and excuse their come here/go away behavior as part of life. You were just a child and couldn't know how to judge how much or how little they had in their emotional accounts, so you took what they had as the gospel truth regarding emotional availability.

When you are ready to choose a partner, you look for someone who matches them and think you are going to get your emotional needs met, but it's not going to be any different than it was with your parents. You didn't understand this before, but now you can add an emotional evaluation to your mate-selection skills.

Learning the ABCs of Emotional Banking

If you are looking for a compatible relationship, check out how much emotional availability each of you has in your bank. You may think that you both have the same amount, but even if it appears that way on the surface, it may not be the case. If he drives a wonderfully expensive car, you might assume he has money, but that may be the extent of his means and he has to go into debt each month to pay all his other expenses. An outward display of prosperity may look like financial availability, but you learn it's not. The same holds true for emotions.

If you have five hundred dollars in your emotional account and he has fifty, there are going to be some major problems. If you think he has enough to match you and he doesn't, you are going to expect something that he can't deliver, and you are headed for disappointment and hurt in this relationship. It's like expecting him to make half the payments on the house you bought together, but rather than contributing his share of two thousand dollars each month, he gives you six hundred because that's all he has. Now you are stuck with the house and are coming up short every time a payment is due.

You keep asking for more, maybe even demanding it; however, it's just not there. He may really want to give it to you and try his best, but if it isn't there, no amount of effort will create it. Or perhaps it's the other way around, and you are the one who comes up short emotionally each month.

You always have to look at both sides of a relationship to see who has what to give.

The saying goes that you can't get blood out of turnip. If your partner doesn't have the emotional investment you need and you think you're going to get support, sharing, understanding, good communication, and emotional help in raising your children, you have a rude awakening coming. It's like buying a small appliance only to get it home and find half of the attachments are missing. When you take it back to the store for an exchange, you are going to be smart enough to check inside the next package and make sure all the parts are there.

This is the same thing you do in relationships if you are a smart cookie. You look at your past emotional relationship with both of your parents and his past with his parents. If there were secrets to picking The One, this would be at the top of the list, yet many people disregard this step. Luckily, examining someone's past to determine what the future will bring is like following bright neon signs—once you know what to look for.

VICTORIA AND ANDREW: FINDING AN EMOTIONAL MISMATCH

As a caring therapist, Victoria was sensitive to other people's feelings and needs and was in touch with her own emotions. When she met Andrew, she thought he was the same way, because he seemed to be sensitive to her thoughts and feelings. He asked her how her day went and listened carefully. She thought she had finally met someone who was completely unlike her not-very-sensitive parents, that she had struck gold. He didn't have a job that required sensitivity and his mother wasn't sensitive, but Victoria figured he had somehow managed to pick up sensitivity somewhere else.

She cared about him, and they talked for hours about his life, his dreams, and his goals. She always wanted to know what he liked best and provided it if she could. He seemed to do the same. Yet when Victoria experienced one of life's downsides and became depressed while she struggled through it, Andrew suddenly couldn't talk to her about her feelings any longer. He started making himself scarcer, and one time he even left while she was crying and telling him how awful she felt.

He had only so much emotion to invest; after that, he was at a loss as to what to do next. There was nothing left inside for him to pull out and offer her. Victoria had mistakenly believed he had a reservoir of emotional availability when he only had a small surface amount; when that was gone, there was nothing left. She was glad she had found that out before making a permanent commitment to him, and although the inevitable breakup was difficult, she came out better in the long run.

Sleuthing Out the Patterns

We all have our own definition of emotional connection, and one definition is no better or worse than another; it's all a matter of personal wants and needs. If two people operate on an impersonal basis and are happy, then that relationship works for both of them because no one wants more than the other can give. They are both on the same page. But if one person wants a personal connection and the other is comfortable with the way things are, it's not going to work well. The partner who wants more emotional investment is going to be seen as the troublemaker in the relationship, always wanting more than the other partner can give. They are no longer on the same page and sometimes not even in the same book.

We've picked up our individual definition of what an emotional connection is and what ideas and comfort zones we are used to from parents. There is a pattern from one generation to the next that will often give you clues as to what someone's emotional comfort level is going to be, based on what he or she has experienced. Many people believe the way their family related to each other was the right way, and they carry that forward into their adult relationships. Or maybe their family's way is all they know. Here are the clues to look for:

• **What role did emotions play in your and your partner's families?** This will give you a clearer understanding of how they are going to play out in your relationship. Who wants and is comfortable with what can be ascertained by checking out what emotions were prominent in your respective childhoods. One family might show only anger, only love, only criticism, or only support. Down the line in your adult relationships, anger may only be expressed when you two are alone, or one partner may be more affectionate when outsiders are present. What you are getting is a mirror effect of the old family dynamics in your current relationship.

• **Were your parents and your partner's parents verbally oriented and did they use words to connect, or**

were they physically oriented, with hugs and touches being a part of daily life? Look at your perception of this. If they were verbal, would you rather have had the hugs; if you got the hugs, would you rather they had talked to you more about feelings? The way this surfaces in later relationships is that hugs are enough for some people because that's what their parents did and that worked for them. For others, a hug only goes so far and then they ask, "What's next? That was a good start, but I want and expect more than that." This is why you need your own definition of emotional connection.

• **What were the priorities in your and your partner's families?** It might have been work or play or discipline or just coasting along. It might have been that the children weren't the priority and didn't expect to be, even if that's what they really wanted. If the parents were very loving toward each other but disregarded their children, you may think that's what a romantic "perfect" couple looks like and that's how your future relationships should operate.

The emotional connection you experienced growing up was the only game in town, and you learned a lot from many years of practice. See if one of the following patterns looks familiar to you.

Past: Parents give hugs and say, "I love you," but that's as far as the emotional connection goes. They never ask what you are thinking or feeling so they can better understand you as a separate individual. They don't ask about your fears or your hopes and aspirations. They also don't sit down with you and have a talk about emotions. The parents are giving all they have and believe that's sufficient. They believe they are showing their love verbally and physically, and that should be enough for you.

Present: You or your mate will say, "I love you," but then run off to do your own thing, leaving the other to handle any emotional needs alone. You've offered all you have or are willing to invest in the situation and don't see the problem if that isn't enough. It must be that the other person wants too much.

Past: Parents do all the "right" things for their child, such as taking him or her to ball games, the park, or ballet class, yet they never try to find out how the child is feeling. It's all about being dutiful.

Present: You or your mate do the "right" things for the other, such as handling the finances, mowing the lawn, or taking turns cooking, but feelings are kept at a minimum. You are being conscientious, reliable and dependable, and you wonder what more can be expected of you.

Past: Parents give a child lots of material things but never make time to be with that child and never show affection or support.

Present: You or your mate believe that if you give the other material things you are saying you love that person and that it is the same as communicating on an emotional level. Things are what you're comfortable giving, but it creates a sense of guilt in the other partner that he or she wants more than that.

Past: Parents stay married for the sake of their children, but there is no love in the house, just a commitment to remaining together.

Present: You or your mate believe that staying together is enough, and you don't have to give any more than that—if you do, it's only for show. Emotion is not a high priority nor does it have any significance or value. Being committed is enough as far as you're concerned.

Past: A parent is caught up in the busyness of the outside world, whether it is work or a social life or a hobby, and has no time or interest in communicating with the child on an emotional level.

Present: You or your mate either imitate this or sit side by side in front of the TV, not knowing there is something missing in your relationship. Your present family is not the priority any more than your childhood family was.

Whatever kind of emotional connection you and your mate find comfortable, know that it will be difficult for either of you to change. He wants it his way because it's important for him to be right, and you want it your way. We all fall into this needing-to-be-right trap and think our way is best. We believe that if our family did something a certain way, that is the right way to do it. It worked in your family or his, and you each believe you turned out OK, so why would you want to do it differently?

The earlier examples showed you how the baton gets passed from one generation to the next and how to look behind the curtain of family dynamics to see what type of emotional bank balance has been inherited. Much of what we know is handed down because we learn by example.

We may want ourselves, our mate, and our relationship to be different than what we saw growing up, but we have to look inside to see how much emotion we have to access. Then we have to match that level as closely as possible to that of our partner or at least find someone who is willing to do the work to add to his account. Of course, if he's the one with more to give, you might be the one who needs to make some changes.

If you are just emotionally surviving each month, how can you invest more than you have? You can't go into debt with emotions; there are no brokers who are going to find you an emotional loan. You only have what you've got—that's all. You may be using all your emotional assets just working and taking care of your family; after that, your emotional bank balance is close to zero. You might have a dollar or two to spend on your relationship, but that doesn't go very far in strengthening the bond with your mate. If you and your partner are both giving all the emotional availability you have and it's still not much, the relationship will eventually go into bankruptcy.

DEBRA: AN EMOTIONALLY BANKRUPT CHILDHOOD LEADS TO THE SAME TYPE OF MARRIAGE

Debra was a highly intellectual woman with a lot going on for her. She had graduated from one of the top universities on the East Coast and had secured a high-level job in the political field. She was going places, and there was talk of her being chosen for a very prestigious position with the government. She was meeting her goals professionally, but personally, there was a lot to be desired. Her marriage seemed cold and certainly didn't hold the excitement that her job did.

While she was growing up, Debra's parents had stressed the importance of money and status, and they made it clear what they expected her to achieve in life. Emotionally, her family lived in a desert. There were never any hugs or pats on the head or words of love and appreciation. Her need for affection was swallowed up by the emotional black hole that existed in her relationship with her parents and siblings. Her wound of emotional abandonment ran deep and affected her throughout her life, showing up in all her relationships.

She had met her husband, John, in college. Although he had already been married and had a child, she felt she had met her perfect match, and they got married. John also came from a highly critical family, and nothing he did had ever been good enough. In the first years of their marriage, they were occupied with raising their three children, and this was always their focus rather than how much they could offer each other on an emotional scale. By the time the children started going off to school, there was nothing left to their marriage except sharing the same house. What had started out as a potentially rewarding relationship had evolved into nothing more than their bodies occupying the same space. After a separation, they eventually divorced because Debra couldn't take the coldness any longer. She wanted more and hopes to find that.

These two were highly intellectual people, and as with many of us, they focused on thought rather than emotion. It's easy to talk about feelings, but it's much harder to be in touch with and express them. That's a whole different ball game. People may be able to talk about things, but behavior is where emotional capabilities prove themselves, so it's an important point to consider in picking a mate or assessing the one you currently have.

Be sure to ask yourself, "How do we match up emotionally? How much do I have in my emotional account, and how much does he have?" before you invest heavily in a relationship with anyone. Look closely at your (potential) mate's parents. He may seem like The One, but until you see what his parents are like, you can't have the full picture.

Sabotage, Anyone?

Sabotage obstructs or hampers relationships from becoming closer and more emotionally intimate; sometimes it destroys the relationship altogether. Sabotage can be overt so you can see it readily—such one partner having an addiction—and at other times, it hides in the bushes so it is difficult to detect—such as one partner demanding that the other lose those twenty pounds to become more attractive but cloaking the demand in the guise of sincere caring.

You may be undermining your relationship and not letting it get any deeper or more intimate without realizing what you are doing. Sometimes sabotage is so subtle that you can't spot it until you do it over and over and then begin to see a pattern. This can happen with a long-term partner or after a few weeks or months of dating to ensure that the relationship goes no further. Then again, maybe it's the men you choose who do the sabotaging; you sabotage yourself by allowing this behavior in your life. If you want to have a relationship that is not parent-based, you have to decide whether you are hampering what you say you really want your relationship to look like. To do this you can go back to what you learned in the previous chapter about fears and see if you are playing out any of yours.

Look at the following questions and see if any of them hit home for you. Sabotage comes in many shapes and sizes, and you may have to stop and think about your current and past behavior to see if you or any of your mates fall under the sabotage umbrella. This doesn't mean that the relationship is doomed, because some people can work their way through these behaviors and come out the other side as better partners. Only you can determine whether one of you is just giving lip service or is really committed to change.

The Sabotage: The Blame Game

Does one of you blame the other for most of what's wrong with your relationship?

THE PROBLEM. If one of you is always holding the other responsible, there's an emotional distance in the relationship. The one who is blaming isn't open to looking at his or her own issues, sharing feelings, and being vulnerable. It's always the other person's fault, which keeps the focus away from the blamer. The one who is blamed feels guilty, retreats emotionally, and doesn't share his or her feelings.

The Sabotage: Refusing to Compromise

Does one of you reject any attempts to negotiate and refuse to make any concessions?

THE PROBLEM. Relationships are all about compromising two different people's ways of being and interacting. In a healthy relationship, this comes easily. In a relationship that is being sabotaged, it rarely happens. If one partner is inflexible and expects the other to go along with the program, there is no room for the second partner's personal identity to flourish, and the relationship remains stagnant. The one who is expected to comply has to give up who he or she really is and become a carbon copy of the other.

The Sabotage: Keeping the Past in the Present

Does one of you hold on to the past and use it to hinder change in your relationship?

THE PROBLEM. When couples keep bringing up negative events from months or even years ago, they can never get past them and move on to what's happening currently. If one partner's current actions are still being judged by what happened in the past even though he or she is trying to act differently, the relationship never progresses. The one who is being judged wonders why he or she is even trying since the other person won't let him or her get out of the role that's been prescribed.

The Sabotage: Harboring Resentment

Does one of you bear a grudge over past hurts?

THE PROBLEM. In this sabotage, it's not what is said, but rather what is held inside and allowed to fester that obstructs the relationship. It's like a long-term silent treatment. The payoff for the one harboring the resentment is having an excuse to stay detached emotionally because of some indiscretion—whether real or imagined—that happened in the past, without letting the other person even know what the problem is. The partner who is at the receiving end of this behavior wonders why there is distance in the relationship but accepts it as is the status quo without getting to the bottom of it and pushing for more intimacy.

The Sabotage: Lacking Accountability

Does one of you tell the other one thing and do another?

THE PROBLEM. This is classic passive-aggressive behavior often demonstrated by doing the exact opposite of what you said you would do in the first place. For example, your partner may say he is going to mow the lawn on Saturday to appease you when he has no intention of doing it; he will later find some excuse why he couldn't get it done. The passive-aggressive partner feels he or she can't live up to the other's expectations, so to keep the peace, he or she lies. The one on the receiving end learns not to trust what his or her partner says. If you can't trust that the lawn will get mowed on Saturday, how can you trust anything else your partner says?

The Sabotage: Promoting the Age Difference

Do either of you consistently choose partners who are either too young or too old for you?

THE PROBLEM. There are some great relationships in which one partner is from a different generation than the other, but there are also people who use an age difference as a reason not to let their relationship progress. They keep saying how this relationship can't go long term because of the difference in ages and then treat it as something not too serious. They don't have to work on any issues that arise because for them, it's not going anywhere anyway so they play at having a serious relationship with potential. It's one thing to accept the difference, but it's another to engage in a May–December relationship when you know it doesn't work for you and you are going to sabotage it in the long run. You may like a younger man or an older one, but you have to be willing to allow the relationship to grow in spite of the age chasm.

The Sabotage: Keeping Secrets

Do you have secrets that you don't intend to share with your partner? Do you think your partner might be keeping secrets from you?

THE PROBLEM. This is sabotage at its finest. You cannot have a healthy, emotionally close relationship if you are keeping a secret from your partner. This secret can be anything—an affair, whether it's physical or emotional; a vice or addiction of any kind; or financial or work problems. Any area in which you are not sharing your whole self acts as a stop sign for true intimacy. The person who has the secret can't trust the other with the information, and the partner on the other side senses something is wrong but can't figure out what it is, which leads to a lack of trust.

The Sabotage: Using Sex to Manipulate Your Partner

Does one of you use sex as a punishment or reward?

THE PROBLEM. Sex is supposed to be a loving exchange between two people in a relationship. If it's used as a tool to manipulate one partner, the loving exchange doesn't exist. The one who is using it for his or her own needs sabotages any chances for intimacy. The one who is being manipulated can't get to first base where intimacy is involved because sexual intimacy is not allowed to exist.

Sexual manipulation can simply be one partner being "too tired" for sex, when really it's because the other one came home late and didn't call, the garbage didn't get put out, or a remark was made the other didn't appreciate and even after a reasonable explanation the other was still angry. The manipulative part is the silent message that if you don't do something the way I want it done, then I'm not going to have sex with you. Sex becomes a tool for trying to change a partner's behavior without addressing it verbally and coming to a resolution that is acceptable to both parties. Sex is often used as a ploy to gain power and control which results in the one being manipulated feeling used, whether it's consciously recognized as such or not. Feeling manipulated builds up resentment over time as there's only so many times "I've got a headache" can be uttered without the other starting to notice there is a pattern going on. The one being manipulated then withdraws emotionally and sexually, and two people are left who are not getting anywhere close to intimacy. They are both playing games and thwarting any opportunity to become closer.

The Sabotage: Inventing an Excuse to Hold Back a Full Commitment

Does one of you say that if the other loses ten pounds or exercises more or gets a hobby you will love him or her more and your relationship will be wonderful?

THE PROBLEM. You can always sabotage a relationship by wanting your partner to be perfect. If your partner expects this of you, he won't ever allow you to measure up. If you do one thing, the complaint focuses on another and never stops. The question then becomes why you are with someone who picks on you like this. You are both guilty of sabotaging because you've agreed that intimacy is conditional, which isn't true love and support at all.

The Sabotage: Talking Behind His Back

Do you tell your partner you love him and then run to your girlfriends and talk about his shortcomings?

THE PROBLEM. Intimacy is hard work, and you are not doing the work if you are using your friends as a diversion rather than addressing what you are really feeling about your partner and your relationship in general. Talking behind your partner's back might help you stay in the relationship because you have an outlet for your true feelings, but you're not exploring them in a constructive way with the right person. Sabotaging in this way allows you both to pretend that your relationship is OK, without having to go any deeper and become vulnerable or see that it really doesn't work.

If your partner finds out you are discussing your relationship issues with other people he's going to feel exposed and vulnerable to the others' judgment. What was supposed to be personal and just between two people now has just been granted an audience. He will feel subjected to someone else's pity, scorn, or laughter at his expense, and no one wants to feel that way. Any trust that was in the relationship gets damaged, and feelings get hurt so that it takes a long time to rebuild the trust that was once there.

The Sabotage: Spending Too Much Time Away from Each Other

Does one of you often go out with friends, leaving the other home alone?

THE PROBLEM. Having outside interests is great and desirable, but not when it interferes with important togetherness time. You don't have to share all the same interests, but there have to be opportunities for sharing outside of the kids or work or family vacations. Those are all needed, but if one partner is always out and about doing his or her thing (whatever it is), the message is clear that the other person isn't very desirable. The one who is left behind accepts the message that he or she is not good enough to warrant much special attention. As a result, the relationship is sabotaged and stuck in neutral.

The Sabotage: Assigning Roles in Child Rearing

Does one of you make the other act as the disciplinarian in the family?

THE PROBLEM. This is the sabotage that says, "You're the bad cop, and I'm the good cop." If you can't work as a team with the same beliefs regarding how to raise your children, the potential for intimacy in the relationship plays second fiddle to all else as intimacy can't exist where there's resentment. The disciplinarian feels resentment toward the permissive parent who isn't doing his or her job, and of course, this is the parent the kids love to be around. By taking a passive role, the good cop is taking the easy way out and forcing his or her partner to be the bad guy.

The Sabotage: Being a Workaholic

Does one of you tend to spend all of your time working, making work a priority over your relationship and family?

THE PROBLEM. The money, prestige, and social standing may look good from the outside if either or both of you are workaholics, but the cost to your relationship in terms of intimacy can be expensive. It's difficult to have the time for emotional closeness if one of you is always either working or thinking about work. This is a great example of being emotionally unavailable. If one of you is utterly devoted to making money or searching for the cure for cancer, the other is left alone to deal with life almost as a single person. Sabotage occurs because neither of you has emotional access to the other. The workaholic never tries to obtain access to the partner and oftentimes the partner is unavailable to have that emotional connection and hence marries a workaholic.

The Sabotage: Expressing Anger

Does one of you express anger in unhealthy ways?

THE PROBLEM. If one person is yelling, stomping around, physically or emotionally abusing the other, having temper tantrums, or going into rages, the relationship is sabotaged when this first starts to occur. There is no way you can have any kind of closeness if you are always on guard, waiting for the next outburst. The angry partner doesn't know how to be anything but a "rager," pushing people away with his or her anger, and the other partner doesn't dare say or do anything to set the rager off. Anger is not an ingredient in an intimate relationship.

Answering yes to *any* of these questions—whether it's for yourself or for your mate—will tell you that one or both of you are sabotaging your relationship. A relationship that is damaged won't have much depth or staying power, as it is stuck in one mode of operating and doesn't allow both partners to mature. You can't have emotional intimacy if one of you is using sex as a weapon or keeping a secret from the other or living in the past. Those are all deterrents to the happiness you can find if you are both willing to look at your intimacy issues.

Finding that some of these scenarios are true for you also indicates that you are caught in the parent trap, because all of these behaviors can be found in your relationship with your parents. You are working out your childhood wounds by wanting to be happy but not letting that happen. It doesn't make much sense to interfere with what you really want, but the wounds and fears from childhood get mixed up with your adult life and cause you to act in damaging ways.

JESSICA: SABOTAGING SECURITY BY KEEPING SECRETS AND HOLDING ON TO THE PAST

Jessica had been married for seven years, but she still thought of her old boyfriend quite often. One day, on a business trip, she was in his hometown, so she drove by the house where he'd lived when they were together and drove past a few restaurants that had been their favorites. She had never forgotten him and in a way still yearned for him. There had been something special about their relationship, and even though it hadn't worked out, there had been some really great parts to it. One of the most prominent was the sex they'd enjoyed together; she had experienced a sexual high with him that she had never found with anyone else. She certainly hadn't found this same excitement with her husband and was actually bored with their sex life. Her marriage was safe and secure, but it didn't have that passion in it she had had with her boyfriend, and she couldn't seem to let go of that part of her past.

Finally Jessica called her ex and left a message to see if he would talk to her; they had parted on unfriendly terms. He returned her call, and they enjoyed catching up with each other. They had always had a bond of sorts, and the sexual chemistry hadn't disappeared. It was still there in full force. They spoke on the phone a few times, and then she suggested that they meet in person. She hoped that perhaps they could resume the sexual part of their relationship but leave their marriages in tact. She didn't feel it was taking anything away from her husband, because she was still going to devote the same amount of time and attention to him that she always did; she just wanted to supplement her own life.

She got up her nerve and proposed her idea to her ex. He said he would think about it. Although the chemistry was strong between them, he decided he was happily married and he didn't want to risk what he had with his wife. He sent Jessica an e-mail and said that he just couldn't do that, as tempting as it was, and didn't feel comfortable continuing to talk to her.

Jessica was heartbroken. What she wasn't able to see was that she was sabotaging her own marriage by keeping secrets. Not sharing her desires for a better sex life with her husband was sabotage in itself, but then she took another step and acted on those desires by calling her ex-boyfriend.

She was repeating the relationship she'd had with her parents throughout her childhood. She was emotionally abandoned by her mother, who was nervous and fretful all the time, when her dad traveled on business (which was often). She began keeping secrets from both her parents and had a separate life when she was out of the house. She became more and more detached from both her mom and her dad. As an adult, Jessica couldn't fully commit to the partner she had because the needed emotional vulnerability was foreign to her in the past or the present. Having a lover on the side, whether it was all in her mind or acted out, prevented her from pursuing a deeper relationship with her husband. Instead, she stayed tied to her past by recreating the relationship atmosphere she was used to—distant, dishonest, and disconnected.

Often sabotage manifests as hidden resistance. You resist having a total relationship by doing something to throw the train off the tracks, because achieving true intimacy is too scary to contemplate. You employ the same defenses you've used since childhood against being too emotionally exposed, knowing they will keep you safe—even though you won't achieve your true heart's desires.

The parent trap is all-encompassing and will eat up the balance you have in your emotional bank. If you don't have sufficient emotional funds, the parent trap will cause you to sabotage your relationship because you don't know how to communicate on an honest level. Both cases harken back to childhood fears and what you were exposed to at your parents' knees.

If your mate doesn't seem to have much of a balance in his emotional bank account or is sabotaging the relationship, you can tell him what you are observing. You don't want to accuse or point out his defects; simply tell him what you see from your side. You can't make him change or even make him want to. Some people are too scared to take the leap. All you can do is communicate and see what he does with the information.

If you find you are the one who is short in the emotional department and are sabotaging your relationship, vow to change that behavior now. Identifying and understanding why you act the way you do are the first and most important steps to changing. It may take some soul-searching and being totally honest with yourself, but the rewards in the relationship arena are tremendous. You may lose an old, comfortable way of doing things, but you will gain a new perspective on relationships and be so much more fulfilled.

6

Love That Isn't Blind

*Learning the Signs of Healthy Versus
Unhealthy Relationships, or What Not to Wear*

It's important to know how to choose what looks best on you in the clothes department so you can show yourself off in the best light. But there are those shopping trips when you absolutely fall in love with a particular item, bring it home, rip the tags off, and wear it the following day. Looking in the mirror, you start wondering why you chose *that* color, and as time progresses, you seem to be pulling here and adjusting there because it just doesn't fit right. So you end up with this item that is the wrong color for you and doesn't really fit well either. You wonder what the heck you were thinking when you bought it. We've all done that at least once in our shopping careers and hope to never do it again. We can prevent it if we learn why the loser clothing didn't work in the first place.

The same holds true in the men department. We may think he looks good at first glance or on the first date or during the first year, but at some point, reality starts to settle in, and we wonder what window our judgment flew out of. The realization that we've made a mistake can come on slowly or it can hit us over the head like a lightning bolt, but it will occur. Often it happens before the breakup and is the reason for the relationship ending, or it might happen down the road after we get some distance and a new perspective. Then we are able to look back and say to ourselves, "Whatever was I thinking? I must have been in la-la land when I chose him."

Michelle was a bright young lady who came to me wondering why she had chosen to date a man for over a year who had a problem with alcohol. She maintained that he was a great guy when he wasn't drinking, but that part of his personality was starting to concern her. There were times now that she was embarrassed when they were out with friends, because he became sloppy from drinking too much. Other people were starting to notice, or maybe she was just suddenly aware of their reactions. I explained to her that an alcoholic probably wasn't the best choice for a healthy relationship because he couldn't bring all of himself into it, no matter how great he was sober. She was starting to take the blinders off and see that.

Avoiding Faux Pas

Just as there are rules in fashion, there are rules in relationship choices. If you want the best bang for your buck as far as relationships go, the following list will help you learn what not to choose. After you weed out the parental issues that are operating in your life, you will want to learn which men don't deserve a second glance. Just like that dress you walk away from because you already know it's the wrong style for you, you'll be able to walk past a potential partner who you know is trouble. If you have ever made these relationship faux pas, you may want to rethink your choices and make better ones, which you can do now that you know exactly what to look for.

Partners to Pass On
- The Pack Rat who's unwilling to let go of past relationships
- The Child who's unwilling to be an adult
- The Manager who's unwilling to share control
- The Firecracker who's unwilling to let go of anger
- The Blamer who's unwilling to take responsibility
- The Pretender who's unwilling to express vulnerability
- The Obsessed who's unwilling to participate fully

The Pack Rat

This is the man who holds on to past relationships; if he's not talking about them, he's thinking about them. Because his parents didn't set proper boundaries, he can't let go when he should. His parents also didn't give him a sense of self, and he needs all the validation from previous relationships he can get. He might say, "Well, Mary did it this way," "Mary liked such and such," or "Mary and I went here on vacation also." Mary is always in the picture, and he can't let go so that the two of you can be the only two in your relationship. Usually he hangs on to the past because he isn't ready to live in the present. Maybe Mary didn't like him staying overnight when they were dating, so he doesn't stay overnight with you because he learned from her that it wasn't the right thing to do. He is still mentally in a relationship with her and treats you the way she wanted to be treated.

The Pack Rat is the man who has too much to do with his ex. He allows her to call him whenever she feels like it and never sets appropriate boundaries on these calls. She drops over uninvited to talk about the kids or some heartbreak of hers or a job issue—something she needs his input on—and he permits it. He's still in the protector role and doesn't want to give up his importance in her life. A woman who encourages this behavior in her ex may harbor an expectation that the two of them will get back together; he doesn't correct her hopes but plays right along with them.

On the other hand, the Pack Rat can reveal himself through negative comments about an ex: "Sue never cooked" or "Sue used to love to beat me at any game we played, and I hated that about her" or "Sue never got dressed up for me." It could be more extreme, and he thinks she's the worst, most despicable person to ever walk the earth. You can see and hear that the anger and resentment are still alive and kicking. There she is, coming between the two of you, whether his remarks are light or extremely negative. In any case, he hasn't fully come into the relationship with you. While he may deny it vehemently, you are with a pack rat who can't let go.

Relationships are challenging enough without having a third party stuck in the middle. You may end up trying to represent yourself against two people rather than one. You might also be taking some of the residual heat that is really directed at her; you just happen to be the one standing in the line of fire.

Look out if the man you have just met or started dating tells you all about the flaky, strange women he's known or the witch of an ex-wife that he's glad to be rid of. He may be doing this as a diversion to fully committing to another relationship or because he simply hasn't or can't let go yet. In either case, this behavior doesn't leave any time or energy for the two of you to get to know each other, sans the ex. What he is telling you if you listen closely is that he's not ready for a healthy relationship at this point. He needs to put the past in the past; however, he needs to do it himself. You can't help him along this path.

In rare cases, if he's willing to work on his issues, you might give him some time and see how hard he's going to try. Then ask yourself if you have the patience you'll need to see it through. It's going to be difficult, and you'll have to give him lots of space to do this. He may decide when he's through that you remind him too much of the part of his life he's gotten over and that he needs to move on to greener pastures without the memories. It's up to you to decide if you want to take that gamble or not.

Any way this behavior manifests, the other woman (or women) are a part of your relationship, so in a way, you're involved in a threesome. It's you, him, and the ghost(s) that haunts the two of you, preventing you from having a monogamous relationship. It may be sexually exclusive, but emotionally it's not exclusive at all. There are too many cooks in the kitchen, and in this instance, you have to have exclusive rights.

Warning Signs
- Lives in his own world
- Has few boundaries around people who "need" him
- Holds on to resentment
- Needs to feel important to others

The Child

You would think that if someone has an adult body, their emotions and ways of thinking and relating to the world are adult also, but you would be wrong to assume this. There are many people who operate at a much younger age than their chronological one. I've known adults who are really teenagers inside and some who operate from an even younger perspective. These people don't really want to be grown-ups and handle all the responsibilities adults have. Their families didn't allow them age-appropriate experiences, so they never had a chance to go through each step to becoming an adult. Their parents might have been too busy living their own lives, not understanding what child rearing should include. Or maybe life was so scary for these people as children that their emotional development was arrested at some point. As adult children, they're still reeling from their childhood wounds and need to stay childish and have someone take care of them or simply let them be kids.

The Child is the man who still wants to act like he's single and unattached, spending lots of time with his buddies at the local hangout, whether that is a bar, a bowling alley, or someone's house. He wants to be footloose and fancy-free—with your blessing. He figures he isn't doing anything wrong; it's just time out with his friends, so why should you care? He brings home his paycheck and wants to let off a little steam. He thinks you have the problem, not him.

My clients Andrea and Bart came to see me because they were having problems in their relationship. They were both avid gardeners and had some other common interests that had brought them together in the beginning. Those were still in place, but Andrea saw that Bart spent a lot of his free time playing games on the computer. Sometimes he would just walk out of the room without a word to her and head straight to the office they had in their house. She would eventually find him there playing what she called his "silly games." It was as if he had walked out of the house without telling her he was going somewhere, and she would be left to discover it on her own. He couldn't understand why she objected to his enjoying himself, but what he was really saying was, "I still want to be a kid and not have to be accountable to you. I don't want to have to think about how this is affecting you. It's all about what I want." Whether your partner leaves you alone physically or mentally, he's still unavailable to your relationship.

Then there's the man who won't take responsibility for himself; he wants you to take care of everything for him, from paying the bills to getting the car serviced to making his doctor appointments. He may remember to go and he may not. It's your responsibility to remind him, even to call him on the day of the scheduled visit. He forgets where he was supposed to take the kids, and as for getting everything on your shopping list, forget it—he sure will. This irresponsible behavior can show up in small ways or large ways, but the meaning is always the same: "I don't want to run my own life. I want you to do it for me." This is not a good sign for an equal relationship.

If he's filed bankruptcy a few times, owes the IRS money for back taxes, or is always having a financial crisis, you also know he's still a kid. I have a client who won't marry her boyfriend of many years because of the way he handles his finances. He never has money, and she doesn't want her credit ruined because of him. She can handle his childish ways in other areas, but she refuses to do it here. She's now looking at how happy she really is with him because this aspect of his personality is getting old for her.

Putting his life on hold until he wins the lottery is another manifestation of the Child. He wants the outside world to take care of him, and he's not going to get his act together until it gives him what he thinks he wants. Untold riches and a direction in life are what he's always been waiting for, and he will continue to wait because he is unable to find these things for himself. He wants the world to be his parent and solve all his problems so he doesn't have to engage as an adult.

Then there's the man who is undependable and expects you to be OK with that. He says he's going to call and doesn't, or he's always late for everything, giving the message that his time is more valuable than yours. So what if you are all ready and have been waiting for him for an hour? He had important things to take care of, and you should understand and not hold him accountable for how late he is or that he didn't call. A child, in any form, is probably not the person with whom you can find that happy relationship you're after.

Warning Signs
- Shies away from responsibility
- Spends too much time with other people or by himself outside of your relationship
- Expects you to take care of him
- Is waiting for the "big event" to move forward with his life

The Manager

Having to be in control is what sets this man up for a relationship faux pas award. He may be a major control freak, or his style may be more subtle and manipulative, but either way, it doesn't bode well for a growing, stable relationship. Healthy people compromise, but not him; it's his way or the highway. Sometimes these men have a military-style upbringing that they carry forward into relationships, expecting and needing that same structure and schedule from their partners. Their parents had the final say in everything they did, or childhood was such a state of chaos that they need to have control as adults so life doesn't throw them any surprises.

At one extreme, the Manager wants dinner on the table at exactly the same time every night, and every Saturday night is sex night, whether either of you feel like it or not. He may use anger or jealousy to control you, or he may try to keep you away from friends and family. There is a line here that can be crossed into physical or emotional abuse. You have to see if this is where his behavior is leading; at the first sign of it, get out of the relationship as fast as you can.

At a lesser extreme, this man doesn't want to control everyday life events, but he does want you to act a certain way, raise the children his way, and accept his lifestyle choices. And he wants you to agree that his way is the best way, no questions asked. He wants to be lord of the manor in what looks like a nonthreatening manner. He thinks he knows the correct way of doing things and usually chooses a mate who will go along with him. He'll have all the answers, and she will depend on him for guidance. On the inside, he's filled with insecurity, but on the outside, it looks like he's got it all together and is able to handle anything.

On the other side of the control scale is the Manager who is extremely nice to you. He'll do anything you want, bring you flowers and gifts, wash your car for you, and always agree to your way of thinking or anything he thinks will please you. You can tell him how to dress or how to run his business and he listens to you, giving the impression that you are in control of him and the relationship. What is really happening, however, is that this is his way of controlling you. He believes, at times correctly, that since you are so charmed by his kindness you will never leave. He wants a relationship and will pretend to give you control to ensure that your relationship continues. Because he is really manipulating the situation, all of his niceties are only superficial. If he wants something different than what you have suggested or what he knows you like, he can ignore your input or desire and do it his way. This may come as a surprise to you because it's not what you've come to expect from him. He is actually completely self-serving underneath his helpful, caring demeanor. When this type of behavior is going on in a relationship, there is no chance for a healthy emotional connection. Your interaction may look personal, but when you factor in the manipulation going on, you can see that it is truly impersonal and all about getting his needs met.

Warning Signs
- Expects you to do everything his way
- Shows anger and/or jealousy
- Is too nice
- Needs most of life to be structured

The Firecracker

Some people thrive on anger, whereas others shrink from a slightly raised voice. Whatever you were exposed to growing up seems to make the difference. If your parents allowed only silence in place of any normal expression of anger, then you are going to be uncomfortable showing any anger at all; if they shouted at each other all the time, then you will probably think it's OK to yell also.

The man who can't control his anger isn't going to be a good catch in the mate department. If all you get is the silent treatment when he's angry about something, you can't talk it out and reach a settlement. If either partner is unwilling to talk about issues, they never get resolved and the underlying anger never goes away. This type of anger is a big part of your relationship, even though it isn't expressed verbally. Patricia came to me because her husband wouldn't talk to her when he got mad. He would go off to the bedroom and watch TV or sit in his favorite chair and read the paper, and there was nothing she could do to make him talk. When he came out of hiding, he didn't want to talk about it then either, because for him it was over and done with. She wanted him to come to therapy, but he didn't think they had a problem. He wasn't yelling or hitting her, so he believed that she was making a big deal out of nothing.

The man who outwardly shows his anger may do so by yelling, screaming, shouting, or name-calling. He may throw or break things, slam doors, or just walk out while he's angry without telling you where he's going or when he's coming back. He may do this on a consistent basis, or he may be fine for a while and then erupt all of a sudden for no apparent reason. With this type of firecracker, you never know when he's going to go off.

To stay in a relationship with an angry person, you always have to be on your guard and aren't able to be who you are. You always have to placate him in hopes of heading off his aggressive behavior. It never works because the problem isn't you, it's him. There is nothing *you* can do to get him to talk if he's the silent type or to calm him down if he's a rager. He has to be the one to seek help in this area.

If you see him as being mad at the world, but he hasn't directed that anger at you yet, know that it's coming some-where down the road. A person can't behave a certain way in one area of his life without it spilling over into other areas. It just can't be done.

Warning Signs

- Angers easily
- Gives you the silent treatment
- Is unforgiving
- Is unwilling to resolve issues

The Blamer

The blamer's motto is "It's always someone else's fault." He never looks at himself to see what his responsibility was when something negative happens. His parents gave him a lousy childhood, school cheated him out of what he really wanted to do, his friends betrayed him, you started a fight, and his children are out of control for many different reasons, none of which are within his control. For him, not taking any responsibility means that he never has to feel guilty. If he never does anything wrong, he never has to deal with any of his issues, because someone else—in fact, *everyone* else—is always to blame. He learned at an early age that if you are the one who's wrong, then you are the one who gets punished or made fun of or made to feel stupid, and he doesn't ever want to be in that position.

Some blamers come right out and say (sometimes emphatically) that another person is to blame, while others adopt an "oh, woe is me" attitude. Poor him, because he can't get a job, can't find a relationship or gets dumped in those he does find, or just can't discover anything he likes to do. You can give him all the suggestions and helpful hints in the world, but he's not going to pick up or do anything other that what he's always done.

Often all the Blamer wants to do is mope, complain, and feel sorry for himself. It would make his life so much simpler if you agreed and didn't try to help him out. If you insist on helping him, he may listen to what you have to say and agree with you, but then he'll go right on feeling like a victim and take no action toward change.

The Blamer can be very covert in his blaming; you can't put your finger on exactly what he said, but you feel somehow he's saying that something is your fault. You might tell him he didn't call when he said he was going to; his reply will be, "I really wanted to talk to you then, so why didn't you call me? I got caught up in work, you know how that goes." He throws this compliment at you and then turns it around so that it ends up being your fault, and if you don't see what he's doing, you end up thinking you are the petty one and there's something wrong with you.

Blaming is a mind-set, and if you accept it a few times, those few times will turn into a lifestyle with this particular man. If he keeps turning the blame around on you, your self-confidence will start to erode and you'll wonder why you feel angry inside. It's best to leave this relationship faux pas on the rack and move on.

Warning Signs
- Never accepts his part in issues
- Feels he's the victim
- Wants you to feel sorry for him
- Makes mistakes your fault

The Pretender

You meet this wonderful man and think he's the most sensitive person in the world. You are quite taken by his understanding and insight. You just know this is the man you've been searching for. You enter into a relationship with him, and for a while you still think he's great, but with time you begin to wonder where that sensitivity went. You saw it in the beginning of the relationship, but now that you've moved down the road—whether you're married or just dating—you're beginning to wonder if what you saw was real. You start to wonder if he's changed or if you misread his true personality. Was all his understanding and compassion superficial?

Men who come across as terribly sensitive may have come from parents who put on whatever front they needed to impress others. It was all about the outward show and pretending to be who they weren't. Some men are truly sensitive; and others aren't but like to appear that way, copying their parents' style. The for-show group have learned that women love sensitive men and have decided that's how they are going to act. They have learned to send flowers, recite poetry, enjoy chick flicks, and love your favorite food. They might even change their diet for you or listen to your type of music or wear a shirt in your favorite color—or at least buy you something in that color. They are the perfect image of the sensitive man, and you may be tempted to accept this image at face value, but you are selling yourself short if you don't investigate further.

Sensitivity has to exist not only in the surface areas such as food and movie preferences, but also on deeper levels to make your relationship real and something you can live with and not be disappointed. It doesn't mean much if he buys you your favorite perfume and then pouts because you never wear that miniskirt he gave you—even though you never wear revealing clothing. The first looks thoughtful, but the second is not about you, it's about him. He may do something extra nice such as purchasing tickets to that play you want to see and then refuse to compromise in any arguments the two of you have. He's only sensitive when it suits him; if it doesn't, watch out. This is not true sensitivity, no matter how you look at it. He might be sweet and kind, but in exchange you'd better let him off the hook for any work that needs to be done around the house.

Some men who act this way do have a certain degree of sensitivity and may be willing to look at themselves and work on developing it further. Others don't have much or any at all; they're just playing a role, and a role does not a healthy relationship make. If he isn't being who he really is, you only have a partial partner.

His sensitivity is conditional, whereas if he were really that sensitive man you thought he was, it would always be there and would show up in all areas of your relationship. Not all the time, of course, because no one can be sensitive 24/7, but the majority of the time it would be present. What seemed at first to be a great attraction may turn out to be only part of who he really is, so remember, you need to look at the total package or be surprised down the road that what you thought was there really isn't.

Warning Signs
- Comes on too sensitive at the beginning
- Has "intermittent" sensitivity
- Is missing a certain depth
- Comes across as too good to be true

The Obsessed

An obsessive man can't be in a relationship fully because a part of his mind is *always* on something else. He may be obsessed with food, his work, or his physical appearance;

the latter resulting in hours spent in the gym each day or just depression about how he looks. It could be sports; gambling; material things; spending or scrimping; or a problem with drugs, alcohol, or sex. He may be in denial about his obsession, but his inability to participate in a relationship is the same whether he recognizes it or not and no matter what the object of his obsession is. The fact is that the addiction keeps his focus away from you and on something else.

Obsessions are usually a result of either too little or too much power and control. If his parents had to have power, they taught him that always being in control is the safe way to live life. If they didn't take any control, then he feels that he'd better so there is some semblance of order in his life.

He might make you a part of this by promising to change so you'll stay with him. Or perhaps he knows you are the rescuing type and will stick with him to try to take care of him in the hope that he'll change. In rare cases, you can help a person change, but the vast majority of the time you can't, because he doesn't really want to give up his addiction. If, by chance, he does eliminate his obsession from his life but doesn't work on what lies behind it, you will have an empty shell for a partner. The obsession won't be there, but neither will he. His body is, but his mind and soul are still lost somewhere, which is why he turned to obsessive behavior in the first place.

If the addiction is alcohol or drugs (either street or prescription), it is going to destroy his body, mind, and emotional self, so don't be fooled into thinking that he's going to be the same guy you first met or the guy you hoped would be your dreamboat. Be very wary if you have even a passing thought that this might be happening. You don't want it in your life or your children's.

A sex addiction will tear down his self-worth and replace it with shame. If you suspect he's obsessed with online porn or acting out sexually with prostitutes or women he picks up in bars, your relationship is in big trouble. You could personalize his deviant sexual behavior and think it's about how you don't measure up (which it isn't), and then both of you are left feeling insecure, worthless, and incapable of a healthy emotional connection. Susan found her boyfriend was visiting porn sites on a regular basis. She had been wondering why their sex life felt empty and why at times he couldn't get an erection. He seemed to be losing interest in sex generally, and she assumed that she wasn't desirable to him any longer. She confronted him, and he admitted that he was addicted to porn. Susan then believed she somehow had to measure up to the women on those sites so he would come to her with his desires and stay away from online viewing. This strategy never works, and his obsession was destroying their relationship by putting more and more distance between them; he had nothing to give her in this area.

If you are with someone like this, you should know it's a long road for the Obsessed to get to a place where he can have a healthy, functioning relationship. There was a wound there in the first place, so first he has to give up the addiction, then discover what the original wound was that he was trying to escape through his addiction, and then face the wound and move forward. It takes people many years to go through the whole process. If you think he is obsessed with anything, walk right past this selection.

Warning Signs
- Is preoccupied with something outside of your relationship

- Is secretive about his obsession, even though you sense something is amiss
- Wants you to try to rescue him
- Has always had some type of obsession

I hope that now you can clean the problem men out of your closet and make room for the relationship that will best suit your needs. Sometimes you have to get rid of an old style before you can pursue a new one. If you are stuck in sweats and want a more pulled-together look, get rid of the sweats and go out and find those clothes that give you the image and feeling you want.

Now that you know what type of man not to get involved with, it's time to turn your attention to the signs of a great relationship. Wouldn't you know it? You can't look only at him; you also have to look at yourself and be able to recognize what you bring into the relationship mix. Remember, it's not all him. If you find that you keep choosing unfit men, it may be true that they are really undesirable, but it's in your best interest to look at how your selection process may be leading you astray.

What's In and What's Out in Healthy Relationships

Looking over the following list will give you an easy way to identify the ingredients needed to make your relationship the best it can be. We'll expand on this further, but for now, see where your relationship falls or where you have been going wrong in the past. Everything is correctable, so if you don't like what you've purchased, you can always return it for something that you've learned works better for you.

What's In

- Having two equal voices in a relationship where all input is listened to and respected
- Mutual compatibility on most fronts
- The 60/40 rule—never giving more than 60 percent in a relationship and never accepting less than 40 percent from your mate (Of course, there will be times when you will give or need more, but that should be the exception.)
- Feeling emotionally safe with your partner
- Having the ability and willingness to work through issues together

What's Out

- Acting out or recreating dynamics from the past that are to your detriment
- Using a relationship to complete your identity
- Abuse in any form
- Inability to fully commit
- Keeping secrets

You need every one of the five "ins" to have a relationship that allows each partner to grow, which in turn allows the relationship to change and grow. You might have had relationships that sat in limbo, but if that didn't work for you, then make a mental note of the five ingredients that have to be there and check for them at the start of any relationship.

Likewise, the five "outs" are fatal to the success and health of a relationship. Any one of them will destroy your chances for happiness with a partner or his with you. You can't be in a relationship fully if any of these situations exists because both of you have to be completely present in order to work together for the best possible connection. If you are not married, memorize the "outs" and run like crazy as soon as you spot them. If you are in a relationship and see that you or your mate are indulging in one or more of them, confront the issue head on and deal with it in as healthy a way as possible.

Molly:
Learning a New Way
in Relationships

Molly was in her thirties, and although she had been in relationships with different men, she had never made it to the stage of wanting to marry any of them. It seemed that her choices ran to men who were good for a few dates or even a few months, but nothing past that ever developed. She had decided that she kept choosing players when one of the men she had dated for a number of months suddenly told her he was getting married and was crazy about his fiancé. That sent her into a tailspin because she had deemed him a player also. So maybe it wasn't the men but rather she who was doing something to thwart her relationships.

She still had the phone numbers of some of the men she had dated and decided to call them and ask what being in a relationship with her was like. She was serious about finding someone special and thought talking things over might shed some light on how she could go about it. A few men told her they weren't really looking for anything long term, and she deduced that they really were players, so that didn't help her. But a few talked to her honestly about what they had observed.

One said she was standoffish and wouldn't let him get close to her. Sometimes when he wanted to plan a date, she would have something else to do and would turn him down. He never knew if she really liked him or was just using him when she didn't have other plans. Another man confided that a friend of hers had told him Molly said that he wasn't very good in bed. Yet another told her that she went out to the clubs too often.

She was beginning to get the picture. She was either picking men who weren't available or pretending that she was unavailable. She was keeping secrets, exhibiting an unwillingness to commit, and recreating old patterns from when her parents neglected her. There wasn't any way she could just walk into a healthy relationship with all of the issues she had.

She talked to a therapist, read everything she could find online, and bought many books about healthy relationships to get a clearer picture of her selection process and what message she was sending out and what behaviors she was putting forth. She learned it was often a numbers game in finding The One, so she started practicing the new skills she had learned with lots of men she met online. She's getting closer to her goal and is enjoying a newfound independence from her past. Her new attitude will allow the relationship she seeks to come into her life, and she is confident that she will chose a good partner and be a good partner herself.

Without all five of the "ins," you can't have an emotionally connected relationship, no matter how much you want to believe you can. This isn't to say you can't have a relationship—that's the easy part. Anyone can go out and find some-one with whom to make believe they have a relationship. Believe it or not, many people do just that because it's really all they want and are capable of having. If that works for both of the people involved and they don't run into problems down the road, then no one can say it's wrong. But you can't necessarily say that it's healthy either.

Now that you have identified your patterns in choosing partners, you can turn away from the past and any parent traps you have been caught in and move toward a better future in relationships. You have gained options in your love life that you weren't aware of before. If you are single, you can watch the men who come into your life and determine whether they suit you or not. Now you know better than to depend on looks or chemistry and understand that the men in your life need to fit with who you are and what you want.

If you are currently in a relationship, you can determine if it is working for both of you. If it is causing some pangs of discontent, you can see beneath the veil to discover what the issues are. After you do this, you need to decide if you want to invest in the relationship any longer or if you should move on. Sometimes that's a tough call to make, so to help you make the decision, read the following section and see if you are in the middle of a deal breaker or if there is hope that the two of you can work it out.

Should I Stay or Should I Go?

This important question often arises in a relationship, and barring major abuse in some form, there is often no black-and-white answer. There may be indicators and warning signs that the relationship is in trouble, and you have to determine whether it can bring you happiness or if you need to look elsewhere. It's not an easy decision, but one that you have to address and can make, as long as you have enough information.

We all have traits, and they are not good or bad. For instance, aggression can be either. If it leads to getting things done, it's good; if it leads to violence or unhappiness, it's bad. What you want to examine is how one partner expresses his or her traits and how the other perceives and interprets them, that is, their expectations of how a trait should be expressed or repressed. You will want to look at the environment a certain characteristic or behavior creates, since the characteristic itself is not necessarily the problem. Rather than putting the blame on traits, you must look at each of your backgrounds to see how traits were expressed in your families. If yelling was par for the course in one family, but fights were never vocal in the other, then there is going to be a mismatch if one of you can't adapt to the other way. That is why you have to scrutinize whether what you each bring to the relationship is compatible. It's also important to remember that what we accept from others is how we treat ourselves. If we believe we are important, we choose someone who also thinks about us that way, but if we believe we don't measure up in some way, we attract a mate who validates those same negative thoughts we harbor. Relationships act as a mirror, and we want to see the best possible reflection looking back at us.

I always tell my clients that there are three entities in a relationship: each of the people involved and then the couple as a whole. Your partner may have a trait that's neutral for him, yet when you put that together with your negative reaction to it, you as a couple may have a problem with the longevity of your relationship. Neither of you are incorrect about a particular characteristic or your response to it, but together you are going to struggle.

If your partner is a rager and you can handle his outbursts with humor, then it's not a problem. However, if you lived with a rager growing up and were scared most of the time, not knowing when the next blow-up was going to happen, then you are going to react differently, and your relationship doesn't have the compatibility it needs to make it work.

One of the answers to your question of going or staying rests with the knowledge that no trait determines if you should go or stay; it is your or your partner's reaction to it. It's like placing sun plants in the shade or shade plants in the sun. Some can adapt, and some will wither and die. It's for you to decide whether you are a shade plant in a sun relationship or a sun plant in a shade relationship and how well you or your partner can adapt.

There are two ways we respond to another person. One way is through emotions and the other way is through our intellect. After reading the explanation of each of these ways and understanding the differences, look at the next checklist and ask yourself how you and your partner handle particular traits. There are degrees of these traits, and you are going to rate them on a scale of 1–5 with five being the highest degree of that particular trait and one being the lowest.

The Intellectual Response Component

Your intellectual response involves acting a certain way because you think you should rather than asking yourself how you really feel. Intellectual responses reflect the expectations of what people are supposed to do, be, think, or look like. Your "thinking" is learned behavior that you consider appropriate; this contrasts with what you feel and experience emotionally. We can give someone a hug, but is it a hug from the heart that conveys emotion or simply a gesture we think we should make under the circumstances, making it mainly intellectual? Our emotions get translated through behavior, so for every core feeling we experience, we also have a way of displaying it that comes from our intellect. Intellectual responses are devoid of any emotion.

These responses are often the first impressions you have of someone before you look more closely. For example, if someone says, "I love you," that can mean different things to different people. It might sound wonderful at first, but on a deeper level it may mean something else. Perhaps there's a high level of emotional investment behind those words, and they mean that the person is able to emotionally commit to the relationship. If that's true, the words are coming from his or her emotional core. Then again, it could only be coming from the intellect and mean, "I'm saying this because you expect it," which is a passive mental or intellectual conclusion resulting from an emotional lack of sensitivity.

Some traits are basically intellectual in nature. They are behaviors that come from an unemotional base. Although the traits in the following list can be either intellectual or emotional, for this exercise, you need to think of them as merely intellectual. Picture a child who has a temper tantrum just because he thinks it will let him get his way. There is no emotion behind it. Now think of a child who has a temper tantrum because he or she is really angry or scared. That's the difference here.

Use the scale to rate how often or strongly you and your partner exhibit the following intellectual characteristics with 1 being lowest and 5 the highest:

	You					Your Partner				
1. Stubbornness	1	2	3	4	5	1	2	3	4	5
2. Depression	1	2	3	4	5	1	2	3	4	5
3. Shame	1	2	3	4	5	1	2	3	4	5
4. Apathy	1	2	3	4	5	1	2	3	4	5
5. Ability to commit	1	2	3	4	5	1	2	3	4	5
6. Affection	1	2	3	4	5	1	2	3	4	5
7. Hostility	1	2	3	4	5	1	2	3	4	5
8. Worry	1	2	3	4	5	1	2	3	4	5
9. Friendliness	1	2	3	4	5	1	2	3	4	5
10. Humor	1	2	3	4	5	1	2	3	4	5
11. Action	1	2	3	4	5	1	2	3	4	5
12. Hope	1	2	3	4	5	1	2	3	4	5

If there is a discrepancy in your scores, it might indicate areas of conflict or it might explain why it feels like the two of you are always on different pages. This isn't always a problem; it's simply one thing to consider if you are facing the stay-or-go question.

The Emotional Response Component

This represents your core feelings, what lies underneath the intellectual components you just rated. These feelings comprised the temperament you were born with and the responses you received to it in your early years. It's part nurture and part nature. If you were born with a sensitive soul and that was supported, it becomes a positive trait of which you are proud. For example, if you loved to write poetry and your parents or teachers encouraged that activity, you will feel that your sensitivity has value and you will be comfortable displaying this side to others. If your sensitivity was ridiculed or discouraged, you will hide that side of yourself. Either way, it's there, driving your behavior.

The following traits are likely to come from our emotional side because a pronounced feeling accompanies each. Use the scale to rate how often or strongly you and your partner exhibit the following characteristics:

	You					Your Partner				
1. Sensitivity	1	2	3	4	5	1	2	3	4	5
2. Anger	1	2	3	4	5	1	2	3	4	5
• Physical	1	2	3	4	5	1	2	3	4	5
• Vocal	1	2	3	4	5	1	2	3	4	5
3. Authoritarianism	1	2	3	4	5	1	2	3	4	5
4. Aggression	1	2	3	4	5	1	2	3	4	5
5. Victim mentality	1	2	3	4	5	1	2	3	4	5
6. Pessimism	1	2	3	4	5	1	2	3	4	5
7. Optimism	1	2	3	4	5	1	2	3	4	5
8. Passivity	1	2	3	4	5	1	2	3	4	5
9. Intense emotional	1	2	3	4	5	1	2	3	4	5
10. Level of emotional investment	1	2	3	4	5	1	2	3	4	5
11. Empathy	1	2	3	4	5	1	2	3	4	5

These are important components to look at because they show who we really are beneath the surface and beyond learned behavior. If you are an optimist and your partner is a pessimist, you may balance each other out or have problems because you always see life in different ways. If one of you is sensitive and the other isn't, you might be able to accept that or you might feel that you're continually misunderstood. If the behavioral expressions and the emotional hardwiring are at odds, they can trigger conflict and cause the relationship to falter. It's all about what you can deal with without the price being too high.

The Physical Component

Next you need to look at the physical aspects of a relationship. Sometimes body language and other physical signs clearly indicate our reactions to emotional stress. If we are intellectually or emotionally in denial, our bodies will store all the negativity we aren't willing to see. You will also want to see if the chronic toxicity of being around someone with negative energy is making you physically sick, which can happen without your being aware of it. Here's your opportunity to listen to your body and pay attention to what it's telling you regarding your relationship.

Use the scale to rate any *chronic* physical conditions that you or your partner experience on a consistent basis yet that allow you to function because you've adapted to and normalized them. See if either of you are reacting physically to stress in the relationship.

These symptoms may have any number of contributing factors, so don't automatically assume that your relationship is to blame for them. Identifying their existence is merely a tool to be used as part of your evaluation of all the aspects of your relationship.

Now ask yourself if your relationship is creating acute physical stress. This stress can fluctuate, appearing and dis-

	You					Your Partner				
1. Headaches	1	2	3	4	5	1	2	3	4	5
2. Stomach problems	1	2	3	4	5	1	2	3	4	5
3. Weight gain or loss	1	2	3	4	5	1	2	3	4	5
4. Anxiety	1	2	3	4	5	1	2	3	4	5
5. Low energy	1	2	3	4	5	1	2	3	4	5
6. High blood pressure	1	2	3	4	5	1	2	3	4	5
7. Facial or body tics	1	2	3	4	5	1	2	3	4	5
8. Change in sleep patterns	1	2	3	4	5	1	2	3	4	5
9. Inability to focus or concentrate	1	2	3	4	5	1	2	3	4	5

appearing from one day to the next. These crisis-oriented reactions leave you incapacitated and can show up as any of the following:

- Becoming tense when your partner comes into the room
- Anticipating discomfort, thus triggering the need for alcohol or drugs
- Throwing tantrums, screaming, crying, and so forth because of a lack of impulse control
- Experiencing a lowered immune system, which results in acute illness stemming from stress and fatigue
- Stuttering
- Suffering migraine headaches
- Breaking out in a cold sweat in the expectation of something unpleasant
- Having shooting pains in the abdomen

All of these may be physical signs that something is amiss in your relationship, or they may be the result of something else that's going on with your body but isn't based on your relationship at all. If you are certain that your mate is bringing on any of these problems, you should get help from a therapist right away.

The Sexual Component

Now look at how well-matched your sexual styles are. For many people, sex becomes less frequent as the relationship continues. While decreased sex drive is common in long-term relationships, there still has to be a basic compatibility between the two of you. Otherwise, physical intimacy may disappear entirely or become rote so that you physically connect the dots but all emotion is left out. For some people, sex was never that good in the beginning, but they thought it would improve over time—which it doesn't always. Other couples start off with a sexual torrent only to see it reduced to a trickle over time.

I liken sex to being at the bottom of a funnel: The issues in the relationship flow down from the top, affecting a couple's sex life. If there is resentment, anger, anxiety, or unresolved issues, they will show up in the sexual arena. Sex has both a physical and an emotional/intellectual side, so look over the following list and see whether you have basically similar sexual styles:

1. Does one of you have a high sex drive?
2. Does one of you have a low sex drive?
3. Does either of you have a sex addiction?
4. Do you love to touch and hug and be physically intimate with each other?

5. Are you sexually turned on by your mate
   - Physically?
   - Emotionally?
6. Are you bored with sex with your partner?
7. Do you have the same preferences about talking during sex?
8. Can you discuss sex and intimacy when you're not in bed?
9. Do you share your sexual fantasies and feel an intimate connection while doing that?
10. Do you each listen to what the other wants sexually and respond physically and emotionally?
11. Is there a shared intimacy between you? Where can you each show emotional and physical vulnerability to the other?

If you want a compatible sex life, then you need to have similar views on the subject or to find a compromise so that each of you can get more of what you want and need. If your views on sex don't agree, this area of your relationship may never meet your needs exactly, but finding a satisfying middle ground may work for you. It's all about what is important in your life and what meets your overall needs best. For some, sex isn't the determining factor in staying or leaving a relationship, but for others, it's high on the priority list.

The Compatibility Factor

If you are sitting on the fence on the leaving or staying issue, look at the level of compatibility you have with your partner. It may not give you the whole picture and the complete answer, but it certainly will give you an understanding of where you are on that fence, what concessions you have to make to stay, and then what your willingness to accept those differences is.

It's a major factor as compatibility is of the utmost importance in a relationship, and explains why your partnership goes along easily or is always difficult. Be aware that all relationships take work—some more than others—and it's up to you to determine how much you are willing to do. Even though the general rule for the healthiest relationship is a 60/40 split, some people are OK with one person putting in 80 percent and the other 20; others may reject a 51/49 division. A more uneven split than 60/40 may not be the ideal relationship for many people and it doesn't allow for growth, but the bottom line is what works for you at your current stage.

People's lives change every five to seven years, and you have to look at what your wants and needs are now as compared to, say, ten years ago. Are they stronger or weaker, and are those needs still compatible with your partner's? Alicia came to see me because she was having misgivings about her relationship. At the beginning, she was OK with each of them being personally independent because she was as busy as her husband was, but now that her life had calmed down, she wanted more time with him. She wanted more vacations together, more common interests, and time for the two of them to talk about feelings. Her needs and wants had changed but his hadn't, and she wondered if she should stay in her relationship and try to work things out or move on to someone else who could more readily meet her needs.

In any relationship some things will be good (that's why you got into it in the first place) and others won't. You can ask for and listen to all the advice you want from friends and family, but you are the ultimate decision maker for yourself.

Only you know all the personal ins and outs of your relationship and what you get out of it.

The following questionnaire will help you determine if you and your partner are compatible enough to have a workable, healthy, happy relationship without a lot of stress thrown in. If you answer yes to any one of the questions, you should carefully weigh the pros and cons of your particular relationship.

- Does your relationship now look like you thought it would in the beginning? What were your expectations? Is it better or worse? Are you OK with that?
- Do you have to distort, justify, rationalize, or even emotionally shut down in order to continue in the relationship? If so, do you want to do that?
- Have you merged into a role and lost yourself just because you made a commitment? Are you bound and determined to stick with your commitment at any cost? Are you operating with a survival mentality?
- Does your relationship include disappointment, frustration, and/or emotional discontent that never changes?
- Can you talk with your partner about normal relationship issues, or does the discussion become combative, confrontational, and destructive?
- What level of emotional investment are each of you comfortable with? Does that work for you?
- Is one of you making constant deposits to your emotional account while the other makes withdrawals just as fast? What emotional balance works for both of you?
- Have you and your partner made a commitment to be exclusive, both physically and emotionally? Do you both agree on where the line is drawn regarding having

a friend of the opposite sex to whom you are emotionally connected?

• Are you and your partner capable of supporting, giving,
  sharing, and relating to each other?

• Have you made a commitment to being engaged fully
  on physical, mental, emotional, and sexual levels?

Ruth:
Changing the Dynamics in Her Relationship

Ruth spent many hours in the chair at her therapist's
office. What she learned was sometimes painful,
but it also brought new insight to the whys of her relationships. She had a husband she liked well enough, but
he let her make all the decisions and pretty much run
the show, just as her dad had expected her mother to
do. She had married her father but found that it wasn't
all she'd thought it would be. Sure, she felt safe in that
role because she had lived with it in her growing-up
years, but at the same time, she was experiencing discontent because she didn't want to repeat her parents'
marriage. She wanted one of her own.

She thought she wanted an equal partnership, yet her
past kept her away from that. She had no role models to
teach her what being equal looked like, so she couldn't
have recognized an equal partner if he sat down right
next to her and said, "Hi." She is slowly learning what
goes into a relationship like that and what risks she will

have to take with her husband to make their relationship work that way. It's all fascinating to her, and she's getting to the point where she's ready to talk to her husband and work on changing the dynamics between them. Hopefully he isn't too set in his role and will be open to these changes. If not, Ruth has an important decision to make about staying or leaving.

Some people take years to make the decision to leave or stay, even the person who comes home after years of marriage and says he or she can't stay any longer and asks for a divorce. Others may talk it over with their partners and see if they can make it work with all the water that's flowed under the bridge; some never make a conscious decision at all, but let life just happen and see where that goes. Perhaps the other one leaves or dies or they both stick it out, all the time not being that happy in the relationship. Others jump out at the first sign of trouble or after a very short time and move on to the next person or decide to go through life alone. It can be an easy decision to make or it can be difficult if the message you got growing up was never to divorce or if you were the one who decided you were always going to stay married no matter what.

You have to be able to live with your decision so think carefully about it. Armed with the information you have gathered from this book, you will be able to make the most informed assessment you can as to the staying power of your relationship and your happiness there. Don't sell yourself short. Always combine your intellect with your emotions so that your decisions reflect the total you.

7

Your Best Shot at Happily Ever After

Being a Winner in the Relationship Department

Being victorious in the relationship arena consists of having correct information about yourself, the ability to assess the people that cross your path, and the knowledge of how relationships work in general. It's like mixing up a cocktail with one part of this, three parts of that, and a dash of something else. Mixed all together it creates a great drink just like knowing what makes a happy relationship creates satisfaction with another person.

Make sure you get the ingredients correct by knowing what to look for and not be in too big of a hurry to just hook up for the sake of hooking up. Love is too important for a rush job.

Love Takes Time to Grow

Know that the wonderful first blush of a relationship isn't always going to be there down the road. As much as we'd like them to hang around, the butterflies aren't going to last forever. We are all on our best behavior at the start of any relationship, but it takes at least six months to a year to really get to know someone. After that, the feeling that you must put your best foot forward fades away and courting rituals are a thing of the past. Everyone starts showing who they really are. Living through life's experiences—the good, the bad, and the indifferent—really tells us who our partner is by showing us how he handles the high, low, and ho-hum periods of life. Remember, love takes time to grow—years, in fact—so don't mistake the initial rush or endorphin overload as love when it's simply infatuation.

Looking at Him Carefully

First you meet him, then you make an observation about him, then you add and subtract from that first opinion as you spend more time together. The rule of thumb is to take a second look, a third, a fourth, or however many are needed to determine who this person you're allowing into your life really is. Look to see if he has dealt with his childhood wounds as you have hopefully dealt with yours. Maybe these wounds are long gone and maybe you are working on them, but at least you know you have them and are trying to lessen their effect in your life and relationships. Make sure he is doing the same and not carrying all his past parental issues into your relationship where they will certainly show up sooner or later. None of us can escape the messages we got from our parents; they don't disappear into thin air just because we want them to. They have to be identified and worked through. Make sure you both have at least started that process and are willing to continue doing the work it takes to eliminate as many problems from your past as you can.

Nice Men Are Everywhere

This is true. There are lots of nice men in the world, but that doesn't mean this one is the right one for you to have a long-term happy relationship with. Many women think, "But he's so nice, I should like him." You not only have to like him, you have to respect who he is, what he represents, and how he deals with you, his family, his friends, and society in general. If you are don't think you can, you are better off passing on him and looking for someone who fits with your needs better.

Now that you have read the preceding chapters, you are much more knowledgeable about the pitfalls of not dealing with childhood issues and how they affect relationships. You have a better understanding of what you need and what type of man is going to satisfy your needs. He's not going to be abusive in any way and he's not going to be immature, but he's not going to lay his jacket down across a puddle so you don't get your shoes wet either. Putting you on a pedestal is not a good relationship practice. If he has already done this, know that you are going to come down from your perch at some point and it's not going to be pleasant. None of us is perfect, but the vast majority of us are not all that bad. We fall someplace in the middle, so beware of the "too-nice" man. This is a pretense that is not going to last; if by some unlikely chance it does, think about how superficial a relationship like that would be.

Separating Mr. Right from Mr. Maybe

If you've been hooking up with the same type of man over and over, he's not Mr. Right or you would have settled on the first one. Perhaps you keep finding all the Mr. Maybes or Mr. Wrongs of the world. Your fears may be leading you to the wrong men, but you can change that. One of the best pieces of advice I can give you is not to settle for something less than what you want—fears or not. It's much easier to look at your fears straight on and work toward lessening their impact on your love life than to be perpetually dissatisfied with whom you are with in the romance department.

Mr. Right is going to be someone who loves and accepts you for who you are, as you do him. He is going to be open to working on his issues from childhood, and he's going to respect that you are doing the same. There is going to be a closeness between the two of you that you have probably never experienced before. Your relationship is going to have its ups and downs, but overall you are going to feel like the luckiest woman in the world to have the relationship you have, and that is thanks to the emotional work you have done on yourself.

Put Your Best Foot Forward

A healthy, loving person with good self-esteem insists on being treated with dignity, love, and respect. You can only expect others to treat you the way you treat yourself, so be especially kind and nice to yourself and recognize your worth in the world. Anything you picked up along the way to adulthood that doesn't support that positive belief was wrong, and you have the power to change any negative messages you received in the past. You have to value yourself so that others will do the same. Once you can place a high value on yourself, you can then place a good value on your partner.

Be certain that your partner is able to do this for himself as well as for you. It has to be a two-way street or the ability to value doesn't exist. Do whatever you must to make certain you are living up to your highest capability and are as truthful and honest as you can be with yourself. If you treat yourself in a positive manner, you will know when it's given by another person and when it's missing because you know what it feels like. You become your own best friend and then invite someone into your life who wants to and can be another best friend.

Bringing It All Together

Relationships have many different levels, and you now are aware of the variety of parts you need to look at so you can pick and choose the best fit for you. You are armed with new methods of participating in a relationship and are ready to continue on with your life in a way that will more likely meet your needs and lead you to contentment in this important area.

The relationship you've always wanted and never seemed to get is now within your reach, so stretch your wings, take a deep breath, and get ready to fly. A great relationship is waiting for you, so know that you deserve it and can have it. Don't limit yourself; instead, reach for the stars and, more importantly, expect to get there.

This book has given you important information about relationships so that you can make wise choices. Armed with this information, you will be savvier about your mate-selection process and have the best chance of getting your healthy needs met. Hopefully, I've put you on the road to a beautiful relationship like you've never had before!

Index